D1099719

ART THERAPY

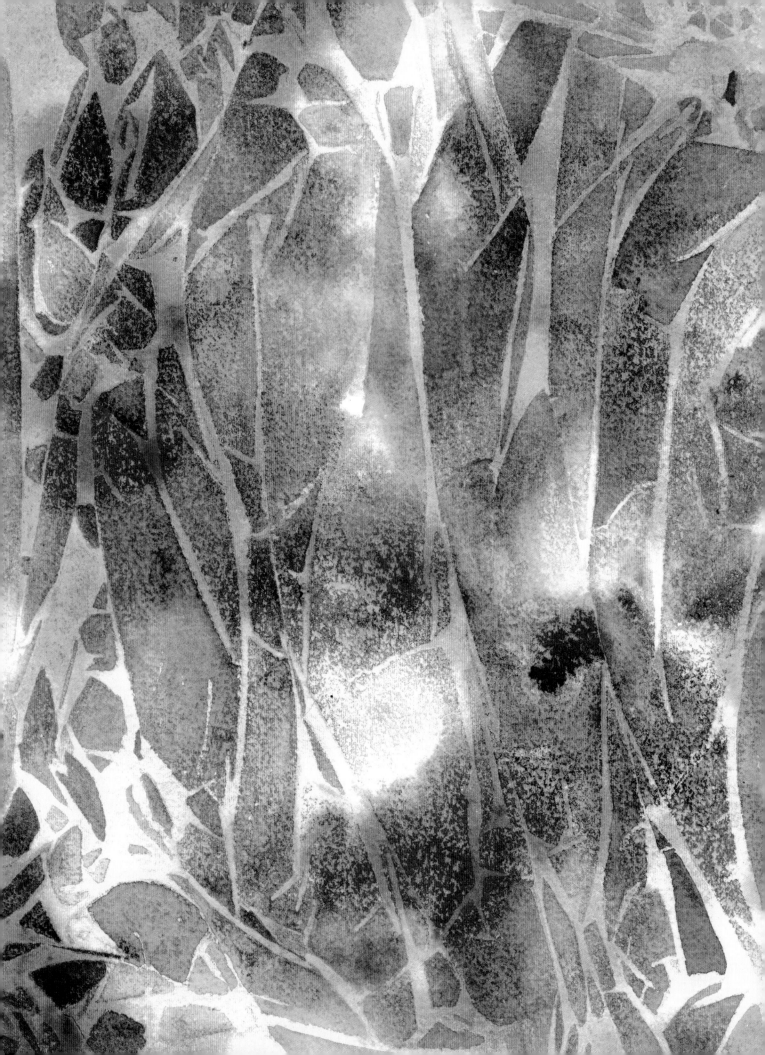

ART THERAPY

CHRISTINE WATSON

ARCTURUS

Christine Watson is a practising artist and further education lecturer. She studied at Winchester School of Art and the Slade School of Fine Art. In 1993 she was the recipient of the E.A. Abbey Award in Painting, with a residency at the British School in Rome. Christine's work is exhibited at galleries throughout the U.K. and abroad, including the Pastel Society annual exhibition at the Mall Galleries in London, where in 2015 she was awarded the Schmincke Prize.

ARCTURUS

This edition published in 2017 by Arcturus Publishing Limited
26/27 Bickels Yard, 151–153 Bermondsey Street,
London SE1 3HA

ISBN: 978-1-78428-580-7
AD005531UK

Printed in China

Contents

Introduction

My ideal way to spend a cold winter's afternoon is working on a painting in the studio with a cup of tea, fan heater on, a good play on the radio, and with luck a cat on the wicker chair. In summer I can open up the studio windows and let in the warm breeze and birdsong, and the longer days mean I can work on into the evening. I switch off from the demands of family life and my job as a college lecturer and let myself become completely absorbed in my artwork. Whatever the season, when my painting day is over, I feel refreshed and invigorated, much like after a yoga or meditation session.

Many people think they can't 'do' art, but I want to show that anyone can, if they try. The motivation to make art seems to be part of the human psyche, for drawing has been a fundamental means of expression for half a million years. Yet while most professional artists can justifiably devote time to their work, the keen amateur can sometimes feel guilty in pursuing what might seem an indulgent activity – especially if it's something they feel they can't do well.

With this book I want to encourage you to make time to be creative. I hope you will find that the process of making art can be both rewarding and satisfying. Mastering new skills can help build confidence and show that different perspectives can help you solve problems – and you may find that, through your art, you can express emotions you have difficulty articulating through words. This has certainly been the case for some of my students, while others have gained more tangible benefits from their new-found creativity. Sharing new skills and encouraging painting and drawing with children and grandchildren has given many mature students much pleasure, while others have started up after-school art clubs; a few, both young and somewhat older, have even been motivated to go on to art school. Others tell me it has enhanced their self-respect to the extent that they have been able to return to work after some years.

The 15 exercises in the book are described in manageable stages, and they should produce delightful results which will surprise you and hopefully impress your family and friends. You will use a range of different materials, some of which can be interchangeable. Don't worry if you are new to painting and drawing as the exercises are intended for both enthusiastic beginners as well as more experienced amateurs. Some of them are quite short and can be completed quickly, while others may take a few days and include options for alternative directions. Give all the exercises a go – I have trialled them with my students and their feedback, in terms of both artistic achievement and therapeutic value, has been enthusiastic.

No previous skills are needed for the exercises, and approaching them with an open mind can be most effective. You will learn some valuable basic painting and drawing skills and techniques that you can use in future work. To help you focus on making your artwork, the exercises are explained in easy-to-follow stages with accompanying illustrations; colour mixing is kept to a minimum and clear templates will help you to get started.

Making art can be both absorbing and calming. Colouring with pencils evokes memories of childhood drawing, and many find the rhythmic movement involved is relaxing. Sorting, tearing and arranging coloured paper is surprisingly satisfying and the novelty of making a collage very engaging. Many of the subjects in the exercises come from the natural world, with beautiful images such as butterflies, autumn leaves, fruit and fields of flowers. You can also produce abstract collages with bright, vibrant colours, and even tackle an upside-down portrait!

Materials

Here is a description of all the materials I used to create the images in this book. Don't feel you have to rush out and buy everything – though if you particularly enjoy, say, the watercolour exercises, it is well worth investing in some good-quality watercolour paints so that you can experiment further. Although some materials may be unfamiliar or seem fiddly, keep an open mind: you may be surprised at what you enjoy most.

COLOURS

The exercises in the book use watercolour, acrylics, pastels and inks. You will probably find you feel most at home with a particular medium for the way it handles or the quality of the colours, but sometimes a subject is best suited to another approach. Try everything – you will be developing your skills while you do so.

Watercolour paints

I use Winsor & Newton Professional Watercolour Paints. In all manufacturers' ranges the 'artist' or 'professional' colours are richer and purer than those of the cheaper 'student' options (called Cotman in the Winsor & Newton range). Tubes of paint are good for making large pools of colour for washes, while the familiar pans of hard paint available in sets are useful for more detailed work. A professional artist will usually have both from which to work.
Terry Harrison's Shadow Colour is a great asset for anyone new to watercolour painting. It is a purple-grey paint that can be used straight from the tube or mixed with other colours to make most shadow tones. Watercolour painting is essentially a transparent medium, so if you want white to form part of your finished work you should leave those areas of the paper unpainted. White paint is rarely used to lighten another colour as it will reduce its transparency and luminosity. Paler colours can be achieved by diluting the original colour with plenty of water. However, occasionally you may use white to highlight features such as the whiskers of a cat or the white caps on waves at sea.

Acrylic paints

While acrylic paints are water-based and are also diluted with water, they have greater covering power and more vibrant hues than watercolours. They dry very fast but there is a wide range of mediums which extend the drying time, flow and glossiness if you wish to develop your painting skills in acrylics. Wash your brushes in soapy water while they are still wet; avoid acrylic paint drying on your brushes (or clothing) as it will then be difficult to remove. You may find that the colours dry a little darker, so try to allow for this when you are mixing colours. I used Daler Rowney System 3 paints for these exercises.

Inks

I favour Winsor & Newton inks as the colours are rich and vibrant. Try out the colours before starting to use them in a painting, as they don't always match those with the same names in other media. You can dilute inks with water, which makes the colours paler, and mix them to create other colours. Inks tend to be less forgiving as they dry quickly and are more permanent than watercolours.
The bottles of ink should last a long time, but ensure that you put the lids on tightly as they can leak – I keep them in a plastic storage box to prevent accidental contamination of my other art materials. Your brushes will be stained by inks, but once you have cleaned them thoroughly with soap the staining won't transfer to other colours.

Coloured pencils

I use Derwent coloured pencils as well as numerous other brands that I have accumulated over the years. They come in a variety of qualities, but generally artist's quality pencils will give better results as they have a higher level of pigment. Keep a good point on your pencils throughout a piece of work. The best advice for using them is to apply the colour in light layers, gradually building up the density. Try to use good-quality pencils as they will blend more successfully if you need to mix some colours.

Pastel pencils

Though similar to soft pastels, pastel pencils are less messy to use as they are encased in a wooden sleeve. Even so, they are prone to smudging, so protect your table, drawing boards and clothes. These pencils are good for mixing and blending and will cover large areas of paper more easily than coloured pencils. I use Derwent pastel pencils and have a tin of 36 colours, which gives a good range. You can prevent the finished work from smudging by applying several light layers of artist's fixative or hairspray (a cheaper option with a more pleasant aroma – though it may yellow over time, so use fixative for anything you might want to keep in the long term). Even fixed work should be protected with a sheet of paper when stored. As with coloured pencils, a sharp point is essential, so keep a good pencil sharpener at hand.

BRUSHES

For watercolours, I recommend a wash brush for large washes and numbers 14, 10, 6 and 2 round watercolour brushes to start with. Most well-known brands of brushes are good quality and reasonably priced; I prefer synthetic brushes as they are firmer and easier to control, especially for detailed work. Watercolour brushes can also be used with coloured inks.

I use well-known brands of synthetic acrylic brushes for acrylic paints. They tend to be firmer and more robust than watercolour brushes and have longer handles. For my paintings I usually work with a combination of a No. 0 and No. 6 round, No. 6 and No. 8 flat and No. 6 filbert (flat with a round tip) brushes; for the acrylic exercises in this book, I used a No. 0 round brush.

DRAWING TOOLS

There are many tools you can use for drawing, ranging from the traditional nibbed pen and bottle of ink to the sleekest modern fineliner. You can even use a twig broken from the nearest bush, or the quill of a bird's feather. The tools you are most likely to begin with, though, are pencils and some drawing pens.

Pencils

Pencils come in a variety of grades, usually ranging from 6H to 9B. H pencils are harder than B pencils, and the higher the number, the harder or softer they

become – for example, 6B is softer than 2B and 6H is harder than 2H. HB is in the middle, so is a good all-round choice. Use good-quality branded pencils. It is important to keep a sharp point on the pencil, so buy a sharpener or craft knife too.

Drawing pens

Drawing pens, or fineliners, are pre-filled with ink and are available in a variety of fine nib widths, usually ranging from 0.1mm to 0.8mm, depending on the brand. It is wise to buy a set of three or four for maximum flexibility. Buy 'permanent' or 'waterproof' pens so that they can be used with watercolour paints without fear of the ink running into the colour.

PAPER

I have used a range of watercolour papers for the exercises, including Saunders Waterford High White 300gsm (140lb) NOT and Arches Aquarelle 640gsm (300lb) NOT. NOT ('not hot-pressed') is an all-round surface, whereas HP ('hot-pressed') papers are smooth and good for finer details. Bockingford 300gsm (140lb) NOT is a reasonably priced alternative for all the exercises. 'Rough' is an option available from most manufacturers that is more suited to looser landscapes. I use watercolour paper for watercolours, inks and some acrylics.

Cartridge paper is most often used for drawing and acrylics, and is available in a range of weights from 150gsm (90lb) upwards. I prefer a reasonably heavy 200gsm (120lb), which provides a good working surface, but a lighter paper can give quite acceptable results.

> The paper weights of 'gsm' and 'lb' are arrived at in different ways: gsm, an abbreviation of grams per square metre, represents the weight of one sheet of paper measuring 1m (3¼ft) square; the pound weight is measured by the weight of one ream (500 sheets), so 500 imperial sheets (measuring 76 x 56cm/30 x 22in) of 200lb paper will weigh 200lb.

You can buy paper or canvas specially primed for acrylic paintings, but I have used watercolour paper or cartridge paper in these exercises.

Tracing paper

Occasionally it can be helpful to make a tracing of a complex image so you can transfer it to your paper. Place a sheet of tracing paper or greaseproof paper over the image, securing it in position with masking tape. Looking through the tracing paper, draw the image underneath with an HB pencil. Then, using a 4B pencil, scribble over the back of the drawing, taking care to apply a good layer beneath the sketched lines. Place the tracing paper, scribbled side down, on the sheet of watercolour or cartridge paper for your finished artwork and secure with masking tape. Draw over the tracing firmly with an HB pencil or ballpoint pen. The image will transfer on to the paper underneath.

An easier option is to place a pre-prepared sheet of transfer paper (such as Tracedown) between your photograph or image and the sheet of watercolour or cartridge paper. Outline the image with a pencil or pen, and your lines will be transferred to your paper. Unwanted lines can be erased.

ACCESSORIES

A few other items are needed for your artwork, none of them expensive or difficult to obtain – in fact you will already have some in your home.

Masking fluid

When you are painting with watercolours you will find masking fluid a useful tool for preserving areas of paper for highlights and finer details which you want to keep white or paint later. The fluid is a latex solution that dries to form a water-resistant layer, acting as a barrier to your paint. Drying usually takes five to ten minutes. You can remove dry masking fluid at any time (after making sure the surrounding paint is dry) by rubbing it with your finger or an eraser to expose the untouched paper beneath. It is available in yellow, pink, blue and white; I normally use the tinted versions as they are easier to see on the paper. When applying the masking fluid, try to think of it as a positive area of white paint rather than a negative space that you are simply blanking out – this can help you achieve a better result.

Handle masking fluid with care as it is hard to remove from clothes and brushes. Set a brush aside specifically for use with masking fluid – preferably an old one. Wet the brush with water before starting or, better still, apply a little liquid soap to act as a protective barrier. Rinse the brush immediately after use to remove as much masking fluid as possible, which will help to extend the life of the brush by preventing it from becoming more and more clogged up. Alternatively, you can use a dip pen and nib or a rubber shaper – a silicone-tipped, pencil-like tool – to apply masking fluid and simply peel it off them after you have finished.

Always wait until the masking fluid is completely dry before painting and similarly wait until the painting is dry before adding more fluid or rubbing it off with a finger or eraser.

Palettes

For acrylics, you can buy a 'stay-wet palette' with a lid which keeps the paints moist and workable for a day or more, though my own preference is for a disposable palette as each sheet can simply be torn from the pad and thrown away at the end of a session. An old saucer is usually adequate for a watercolour palette, but if you wish to buy a palette I recommend one with a folding lid which helps to contain the paint and can preserve your colour mixes for the next session.

Eraser

A soft natural or synthetic rubber eraser, or a firmer plastic eraser, is an essential tool. I occasionally use a battery-operated eraser to remove finer details. Putty rubbers can be moulded to give a fine point for accurate erasing and they are less likely to damage the surface of the paper, but they can be difficult to keep clean. Erasers on the ends of pencils tend to be hard and collect dirt, so they are best avoided.

Extras

Other items you will find useful are scissors; a pencil sharpener or craft knife; a ruler; a drawing board to support your paper; tissue paper; kitchen towel; two pots for water, one for rinsing brushes while working and another for clean water washes (jam jars or yoghurt pots are fine); masking tape (which is more easily removed than sticky tape); and cocktail sticks.

Flower Border

A decorative scene in pen and coloured pencils

Flowers make beautiful subjects and can help you feel in touch with nature while you paint, especially if you spend time in a garden for inspiration. Gardeners use the textures and colours of plants in much the same way that an artist works with paint, so you'll often find that a garden border is a ready-made pleasing composition.

The tradition of painting gardens as a subject rather than as a mere background is comparatively recent. The Impressionist artists produced some of the most memorable images; Claude Monet notably made his own beautiful garden at Giverny the subject of many paintings.

To prepare you for this exercise, we begin with some examples of pen and line techniques which illustrate the broad range of possibilities in this medium. It can seem intimidating to put marks down on paper that can't be erased, but with a little practice, patience and planning it can be very rewarding and absorbing. Take time to experiment with mark-making before you start the main exercise.

Writing with a pen is a skill familiar to most people, and doodling – just a short step away from drawing – can help you get over any nervousness with the pen. Pens and paper are easily available and very portable, so this is a good option when you want to make a sketch outdoors or on holiday. Pen and line also combines very effectively with watercolours and coloured pencils, as this exercise will demonstrate.

You will start this picture in pencil, follow that with pen and line and then finish off with coloured pencils. Colouring in with these immediately takes us back to childhood. The rhythmic movement is very relaxing and the limited selection of colours simplifies any decisions that need to be made regarding colours and gives a unity throughout the picture. Creating a bright, summery picture can be very uplifting, making the exercise a happy experience.

Therapeutic benefits

- Easy exercise with attractive results
- Colouring can be relaxing and absorbing
- Evokes memories of summer days and holidays
- Encourages appreciation of the beauty of nature
- Requires patience and steady concentration.

Practice exercises in pen

The first stage in the exercise is to familiarise yourself with using a pen and to appreciate the wide range of textures and marks that can be achieved. Instinctively, you will start by using the pen as if you are writing, but try a looser grip. By working through the examples here you will discover a huge variety of dots, dashes and lines that you can use in your drawing. The more you practise and experiment, the more options will become evident.

The second example demonstrates how this new vocabulary of marks can be translated into drawings of trees, flowers and leaves. Work through these to explore further the possibilities of pen as an exciting drawing medium.

Materials

A4 sheet of 200gsm (120lb)
cartridge paper

Tracing paper

HB pencil

Soft or plastic eraser

Pencil sharpener

0.5mm and 0.1mm drawing pens

Coloured pencils

Lemon Cadmium

Orange Chrome

Deep Cadmium (yellow)

Deep Vermilion

Deco Pink

Scarlet Lake

Magenta

Imperial Purple

May Green

Indigo Blue

Grass Green

Olive Green

Mineral Green

Jade Green

Ivory Black

This garden border includes a wonderful variety of coloured flowers and distinctive textured leaves. If you can't access a garden to take your own photograph, the internet is a wonderful source of imagery. I have chosen colours from an assortment I have gathered over the years, as well as from the Derwent range.

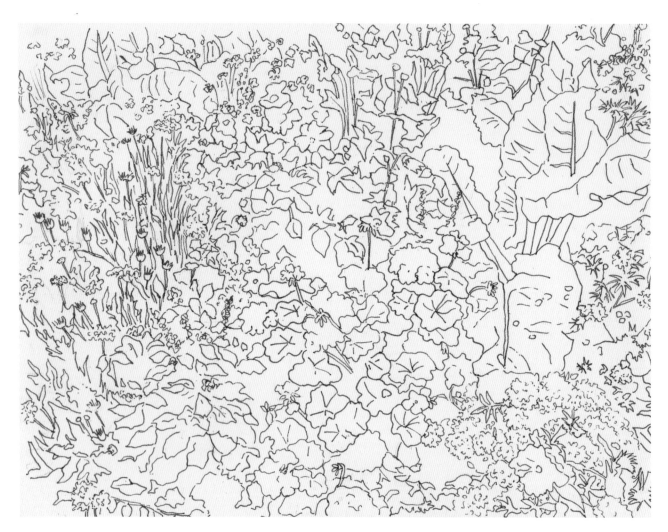

To help you get started you can make a tracing of the line drawing here and then transfer it to your cartridge paper, using the tracing technique on page 9. I have used a drawing pen for clarity. Alternatively, sketch out your own drawing, either from a photograph or from life.

Draw over the pencil lines with your pen, first picking out the main features and then adding in the finer details. Try to experiment with your pen to make as wide a variety of textures and marks as possible, referring to the steps at the beginning of this exercise. Don't worry if you think you have made a mistake – chances are you will be the only person who is aware of it. If you have several widths of nib available, try to interchange them, using the broader ones for the main shapes and the finer ones for more detailed areas. I used a 0.5mm nib for the main shapes and a 0.1mm for finer details.

Don't feel you have to put in everything that you see at this stage; it's often easier to add in details after you have started to place the colours, so keep your pens close at hand. Before you begin colouring, however, take a clean eraser and remove all your pencil lines – you will be surprised how much crisper and fresher your picture will look already.

2 Referring to the photograph, try to match the colours as best you can – you may blend them if necessary, but keep this to a minimum or they will lose their liveliness. Clearly, the bigger the range of colours you equip yourself with, the more options you will have to choose from. Start off lightly and place the most prominent area of colour first. I began with the reds and yellows and followed with pinks and greens. These provided excellent 'landmarks', helping me to identify the position of other flowers and leaves. A dark blue works well for the background areas. You may instinctively select black for the darkest areas, but try to resist this as it can appear dull and heavy. If you don't seem to have the right colour, accept the best possible compromise – it's much more important that the colours work comfortably together throughout the whole picture.

3 Continue to add more light layers of colour until you have almost covered the whole picture. This will take time, so be patient. The result will be brighter and fresher if you don't precisely match the colours to the pen lines, so don't worry about overlapping. For similar reasons, there's no need to make the picture look too realistic as your main aim is a lively impression.

4   Once you have placed the initial colours, strengthen
    their intensity by gently adding more layers. Avoid
pressing too hard since the result may end up looking
patchy and uneven. Continue to use the blue for the
background. You may add a little black to deepen the blue
and purple in some areas. You can always put in extra pen
marks and textures as I have done in the last stage, but don't
be afraid of leaving traces of white paper since this will
introduce freshness and light to the finished work.

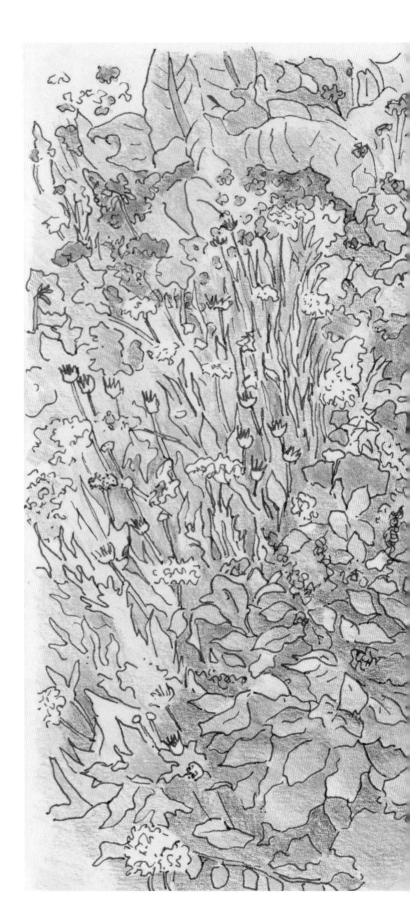

Party Ring Biscuits

A fun exercise in pencil and coloured pencils

This exercise is good for developing drawing skills and confidence. You might not think of biscuits as an obvious subject for drawing, but why not? You don't have to go far to find interesting subject matter, and biscuits are a familiar, uplifting choice. Party rings are a great subject as the variety of colours of the base icing and overlaid stripes add another element of interest. You will learn some basic rules about drawing a circle in perspective without getting too embroiled in the technical theory. The finished result is a pretty pastel-coloured drawing.

Coloured pencils, or crayons, are widely available and you may even have some at home, so getting organised should be easy. Try using the direction of your marks to describe the contours of the object you are colouring in; for example, shade across the flat tops of the biscuits but use vertical lines to indicate the central hole. If you don't have a full range of coloured pencils just do the best you can with what you have; it is possible to blend colours to get closer to those of the subject, but avoid over-mixing as they can lose their freshness. I mostly used Derwent coloured pencils, along with a few other brands in my collection. The cartridge paper here is 200gsm (120lb) as heavy paper will receive the pencil better.

Therapeutic benefits

- Colouring with pencils can be very relaxing
- Reminiscent of childhood, it encourages a sense of fun and humour
- Mastering ellipses is confidence-building.

Drawing an ellipse

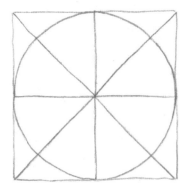 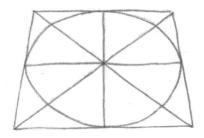 

An ellipse is the shape you see when you look at a circle other than flat-on. The circle will appear squashed to a greater or lesser degree, depending upon your angle of view.

To make a perfect circle, first draw a square and then carefully add centred horizontal and vertical lines, followed by the diagonals. These lines will all cross in the exact centre of the square. Mark a point on each diagonal line that equates to the length of a horizontal or vertical line from centre to outside edge. Join all these points in a gentle curve to form a circle.

Ellipses can be a challenge to draw, but if you bear in mind the following points you should find it possible. First, an ellipse is all curves, with no corners. Secondly, the curve at the front is usually slightly deeper than the curve at the back – the ellipse is symmetrical horizontally but not vertically. Look at the perspective diagram and you will see that the point where the diagonal lines cross is shifted slightly to the back.

Before attempting to draw ellipses, it is worth warming up by making a series of 'lazy 8' shapes. Hold your pencil loosely, about halfway down the shaft, and draw continuous figure-of-8 loops as you move down the paper. If you clasp it too tightly and too near the tip the smooth flow of the ellipse will be lost.

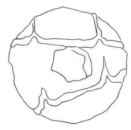 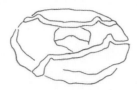

The drawing of the party ring biscuit shows you how you can translate this theory into practice without getting involved in complex geometry. The aim is to give the impression of the biscuit flat on a surface, seen at an angle.

Materials

A4 sheet of 200gsm (120lb)
cartridge paper

HB pencil

Soft or plastic eraser

Pencil sharpener

Coloured pencils

Straw Yellow

Magenta

Deep Cadmium (yellow)

Deco Pink

Terracotta

Rose Pink

Crimson Lake

Blue Violet

Peach

Dark Violet

Imperial Violet

Spectrum Blue

Salmon Pink

Prussian Blue

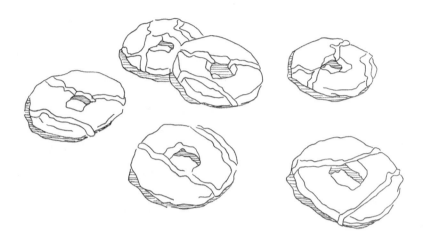

1 Arrange your biscuits, overlapping some of them for added interest. Draw them in pencil, measuring carefully. Notice the spaces between the biscuits to help you position them. Lightly draw in the pattern and then very gently 'hatch' (draw roughly equidistant lines) to show the shadows cast by the biscuits on the paper. I have drawn my version in pen for clarity.

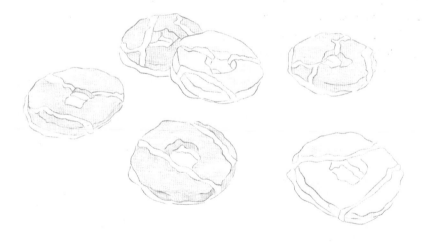

2 Using your coloured pencils, gently hatch in the basic colours of each biscuit, keeping the marks even to suggest the flatness of the surface. Use vertical lines to indicate the depth. Avoid making circular marks that go round the centre holes as this could make them look like doughnuts.

3 Place a bluish-purple colour in the shadows, using horizontal lines which will
   describe the flat surface of the paper on which the biscuits are placed. Carefully
erase excess HB pencil marks.

4 Strengthen the colours, keeping the marks even and consistent. It is possible
   to mix the colours of the pencils to make them more accurate and richer, but
always be gentle. Stronger marks may be hard to soften and may not blend in with
the other colours.

5 Strengthen the shadows to create more depth. A dark blue on top of the purple will give a rich grey. Introduce hints of the colour of the icing into the shadows to increase richness. This reflected colour will also connect the subject with its shadow. Try to avoid using grey, brown or black as these will dull down the image and make the shadows look heavy and lifeless. Don't be tempted to put on too many layers of coloured pencil as the colours may lose their freshness and the picture may look overworked.

Autumn Leaves

A seasonal exercise in watercolour

In the autumn months, nature shows us an extraordinary palette as deciduous leaves change colour and fall from the trees. Walking through woodlands, especially on a cold, frosty morning, can be a very uplifting experience. As the weeks pass and winter approaches, there is a subtle shift in the colours, from green to red, yellow and brown. The stunning intensity of the hues and tones provides a wealth of inspiring subject matter for artists and illustrators.

This exercise will guide you through the simple stages of painting autumn leaves in watercolour. After you have worked through the different examples you should have gained the confidence to work independently and paint leaves that you have collected yourself.

The painting method is simple; if you have the colours listed, or a reasonable match, you only need to dilute them with water to the required strength – you won't need to mix any new colours on the palette. In the process you will pick up the basic watercolour techniques of painting both wet-into-wet and wet-on-dry. I suggest experimenting on a spare piece of paper before starting your main painting. This is a good discipline for all watercolour paintings as you will learn how to control the strength and tonal value of the finished colours. The final result should not aspire to be a precise botanical study but will instead give an impression of the leaf in front of you, conveying the typical characteristics of autumn.

MAKE A COLLAGE

Once you are confident with the basics, you can develop your technique and create exciting colour combinations and compositions such as the collage shown on the facing page. You can either enlarge this line drawing of the three leaves and paint them, or else simply paint three separate leaves, then cut them out individually and paste them down in a pleasing arrangement on a white or coloured background.

Alternatively, make a drawing of several different leaves and paint the composition and background using your new watercolour skills.

Therapeutic benefits

- Vibrant, uplifting colours
- Satisfaction in mastering basic watercolour techniques
- Easy confidence-building exercise
- Impressive results using transferable watercolour skills
- Discovering that less is often more.

Materials

A4 sheet of 425gsm (200lb) NOT watercolour paper

HB pencil

Soft or plastic eraser

Cocktail stick

Toothbrush

No. 10 and No. 2 round watercolour brushes

Watercolour paints

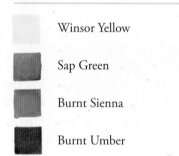

Winsor Yellow

Sap Green

Burnt Sienna

Burnt Umber

Plane tree leaf

There is a line of plane trees along the street in which I live, and every year I look forward to their extraordinary colours as summer turns to autumn.

1 Using the example shown, draw the outline of the leaf in pencil on the watercolour paper. Sketch in the main veins, observing closely how they are positioned as every leaf is different. Correct any mistakes with your eraser as you go. When you draw your own leaves in the future, you can either simply draw around them or take a photo and trace the image from a print – it will make the task easier.

2 Carefully wet the whole leaf within your pencil outline with clean water, using the No. 10 brush. Then add a brush full of diluted Winsor Yellow on your leaf, letting the paint run in the water. The final colour will dry lighter than that on your palette as the paint will be diluted by the water on the paper. Look carefully at the example to see roughly where to place the colour.

3 Let your painting dry completely, which should take about five to ten minutes, depending on the temperature in the room. This will help avoid unwanted patchy effects that can result from painting over wet paint. Wet the whole leaf again with clean water and apply a brushload of diluted Sap Green, letting the pigment run unevenly into the water over the yellow but not fully covering the leaf. Again, the colour will dry lighter so you may want to start with a stronger mix with less water than you used for the yellow. To achieve a clean, sharp edge to the leaf, use the No. 2 brush to tease the water or diluted colour right up to the pencil outline of the leaf. This is to avoid leaving any unsightly hard lines or 'tide' marks in the body of the leaf which may spoil the soft, blended appearance. Let the leaf dry completely again.

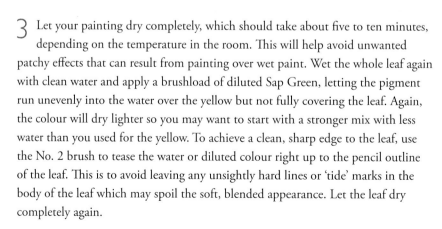

4 Wet the whole leaf for a third time with clean water and apply Burnt Sienna, letting the pigment run unevenly in the water. As you now have several layers of paint on the paper, try to avoid over-brushing as you may make streaks in the paint. You should just gently 'tickle' the surface of the paper with your brush. Let the leaf dry completely yet again.

5 Carefully wet the whole leaf again with clean water. Using a cocktail stick, score carefully along the veins, making a light groove on the surface of the paper. Mix Burnt Umber and a little water and, using the No. 2 brush, paint along the score marks. Use the tip of the brush, letting the pigment run into the grooves as well as bleeding a little either side into the main body of the leaf. Before the water wash dries, add more Burnt Umber to the tips of the leaves and allow this to run softly into the leaf.

6 When the paint is dry, put some Burnt Umber and Sap Green separately on to your palette and add a little water to each. Dip the toothbrush in one of the colours and, by running your fingernail across the bristles, splatter the leaf to add texture and detail (you might want to practise this first on a spare sheet of paper). Don't worry if some of the dots splatter beyond the leaf on to the background. Repeat this with the other colour.

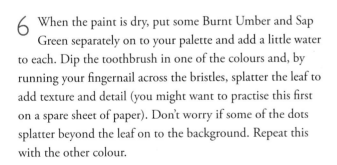

Maple leaf

If you ever thought brown was a dull colour, look out for maple trees in autumn, when their leaves put on a wonderful display of countless variations, from copper to umber. Follow these stages carefully as some are a little different from those in the previous exercise.

Materials

A4 sheet of 425gsm (200lb) NOT watercolour paper

HB pencil

Soft or plastic eraser

No. 10 and No. 2 round watercolour brushes

Masking fluid

Pen and nib

Toothbrush

Watercolour paints

Raw Sienna

Burnt Umber

Perylene Maroon

Perylene Violet

1 Draw the leaf in pencil as in the template. Complete the outline first and then look closely at the veins and draw them in, taking care to draw exactly what you see rather than what you think you see. Use your eraser to correct any mistakes.

2 Wet the whole leaf with clean water using the No. 10 brush and apply a dilute mixture of Raw Sienna, letting the pigment run in the water. Try to leave some white areas close to the veins by carefully applying small dabs of paint about 1cm (½in) away from the veins and you should find that these don't flow so much.

3 Let the leaf dry completely, as you are going to apply masking fluid which needs a dry base so it can be easily removed. Use the pen and nib to draw thin lines of masking fluid along the veins.

Let the masking fluid dry – if you try to paint on wet masking fluid it will transfer to your brush and could ruin it. Carefully wet the whole leaf again with clean water using the No. 10 brush and then apply Burnt Umber. Let the pigment run unevenly in the water over the yellow but without fully covering the leaf. Allow the leaf to dry.

4 Carefully wet the whole leaf again with clean water using the No. 10 brush and then apply some dilute Perylene Maroon. Let the pigment run unevenly in the water over the yellow and brown but without fully covering the leaf. Allow the leaf to dry.

5 Wet the whole leaf again with clean water and then, using the same brush, apply brushloads of fairly strong Perylene Violet and Burnt Umber to the edges of the leaf and let the colour run a little into the body. As the paint will be more concentrated it will not run as far as the layers in earlier stages. If the colour seems a little pale, use the No. 2 brush with a stronger mix to the wet edge and let this run, letting the pigment run unevenly in the water. Allow the leaf to dry again.

6 When the paint is fully dry, rub off the masking fluid with your finger. Add a light tint of Raw Sienna with the No. 2 brush if you want to soften the white lines of the veins.

7 When the paint is dry, use a toothbrush to splatter Burnt Umber and Perylene Violet separately on to the leaf to add texture and detail.

Materials

A4 sheet of 425gsm (200lb) NOT watercolour paper

HB pencil

Soft or plastic eraser

No. 10 and No. 2 round watercolour brushes

Masking fluid

Pen and nib

Watercolour paints

 Indian Yellow

 Scarlet Lake

 Sap Green

 Burnt Umber

Oak leaf

Oak trees provide year-round interest with magnificent foliage in the summer and majestic bare branches in winter. They are usually extremely long-lived and provide habitats for all kinds of birds and insects. Watching branches sway in the wind is not unlike looking at the movement of the sea, and can be extremely relaxing as we contemplate nature's amazing beauty.

1 Draw the oak leaf with the HB pencil, following the template. Start with the curvy outline and then look carefully at the positions of the veins and draw them in.

2 Using the No. 10 brush, wet the whole leaf with clean water and apply Indian Yellow, allowing the pigment to run in the water.

3 Let the leaf dry completely and then apply a thin line of masking fluid with the pen and nib for the central vein. Allow the masking fluid to dry.

4 Wet the whole leaf with clean water and apply Sap Green, allowing the pigment to run in the water. Let the leaf dry.

5 Wet the whole leaf with clean water and apply Scarlet Lake, allowing the pigment to run in the water. Leave to dry.

6 Rub off the masking fluid with your finger and apply a light wash of Indian Yellow mixed with Burnt Sienna along the central veins with the No. 2 brush.

The Colour Wheel

Learn about colour using paper collage

While you don't need to embrace all the scientific complexities of the colour wheel to make interesting pictures, you will find the basic principles extremely useful. I painted some sheets of coloured paper that I used throughout this exercise. By preparing these in advance you will have the freedom to experiment with colour combinations and motifs without worrying about the challenges of mixing specific colours while you are making your collage. Cutting and sticking can be tremendous fun and you can really let your imagination take over. The following exercises are quick and easy, allowing you to have the freedom to experiment with your new knowledge. You could even try to produce pictures that reflect your moods and emotions.

It's useful to understand some of the basic characteristics of colour.

Primary colours are red, blue and yellow. These cannot be mixed but every other colour can be mixed from them.

Secondary colours are purple, green and orange. They are mixes of two primary colours: red/blue, yellow/blue and yellow/red respectively.

Tertiary colours can be found between each primary and secondary colour. These are red-purple, blue-purple, blue-green, yellow-green, yellow-orange and red-orange.

It is very easy to make your own colour wheel using watercolours or acrylics. Here I have made one using shapes cut from self-coloured paper and glued on to a sheet of cartridge paper. I have used some of the left-over paper to produce a few colour theory exercises and collages.

Therapeutic benefits

- Colouring and sorting paper is an absorbing exercise
- The tactile process of cutting paper is enjoyable and relaxing
- Cutting rather than drawing shapes encourages us to be creative with form and composition
- Sticking coloured paper takes us back to school days.

Materials

A4 sheet of 200gsm (120lb)
cartridge paper for the base (if
you plan to do all the exercises
you will need eight sheets in total)

12 x A4 sheets of lighter cartridge
paper for self-colouring

Scissors

PVA glue

Glue spreader and an old plate (or
similar)

Acrylic paints (you can buy
reasonably priced sets of about
12 acrylic colours which will be
perfect for this project)

Acrylic painting brushes

Making a colour wheel

Paint 12 sheets of paper in the following colours: yellow, yellow-orange, orange,
red-orange, red, red-purple, purple, blue-purple, blue, blue-green, green and green-
yellow. Use my example to match up the colours. Don't worry too much if the
colours are uneven.

Find a plate that will fit on your sheet of A4 200gsm (120lb) paper and draw
round it. The circle will enable you to arrange coloured squares in a neat, regular
format. Cut out a 2cm (¾in) square of each colour. When you have cut out one
square you can use it as a template for the rest. If you want to achieve a neater result
you can use a ruler and pencil to draw the squares first.

Arrange your coloured squares around the circle in the sequence above and
carefully paste them down.

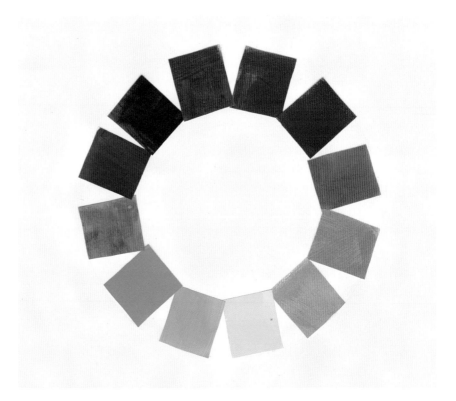

Now that you have your colour wheel you will discover a few useful facts about the
characteristics of colour.

Reds, oranges and some yellows are warm colours while blues, greens and some
purples are cool.

Reds and oranges remind us of fire, heat and summer. They are strong and
dominant and can suggest passion, assertiveness and energy. Blues are cooler and are
associated with the sea, sky or winter. They tend to be calming and peaceful. Greens
are linked with growth and the natural world, and can suggest a sense of peace and
meditation. Yellows can be very intense and they are the most eye-catching in
the spectrum.

Complementary colours

Colours adjacent to each other on the colour wheel tend to blend well and look harmonious. Colours opposite each other compete and bring one another to life. These are called complementary colours. The pairings are red/green, yellow/purple and orange/blue. If you want to find the exact complementary of any colour, paint a dot of the colour on a white sheet of paper and stare at it until a white ring seems to appear around the dot. Then, looking at a white area on the paper, blink and you will see traces of the opposite colour.

Now try the following exercises. Cut out shapes in three harmonious colours, arrange them together on paper and then stick them down as in the examples. Repeat this with the same colour combination, but this time add a small piece of a complementary colour and paste it down. You'll see that it immediately brightens up the harmonious colours.

Complementary colours, also known as accent colours, can bring a painting to life. Look through art books and see if you can find the accent colours in different paintings. You will see them too in magazines; advertisements use accent colours with great skill to enhance images and make products look more attractive.

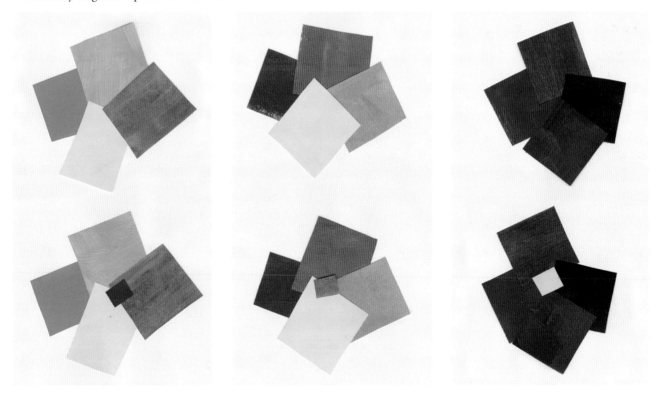

I have also included two examples using the same accent colour on four different backgrounds. Notice how the accent colour seems bolder and stronger on some backgrounds while it hardly shows on another. Try this out for yourself with a range of combinations of your coloured paper and see how the colours interact.

An abstract collage

Use your new knowledge of colour in the next task. Cut out a variety of shapes and colours and stick them together to create an abstract collage.

Arrange your shapes on the paper before sticking them down. First decide where your larger pieces of paper look best and consider how you make a balanced composition. Move the shapes around as you may find that a more exciting composition unfolds as you work. I placed circles at the top and bottom with the rectangles in the middle. The yellow half circle at the bottom leads the eye into the picture as it moves round the orange circle. I used the long, thin purple strips to link the middle shapes together. And I added some smaller details with the red triangles, overlapping them on the green and orange rectangles. The three purple squares on the yellow semicircle echo the purple strips without being exactly the same.

A figurative collage

Make a 'figurative' collage, cutting out simplified shapes of
real objects and arranging them together to make a picture.
The shape you are left with after cutting out a motif can be
used to extend the depth and perspective in your picture. I
have used this device with the fish and reeds in my example.
Cutting out shapes with scissors, without pre-drawing, can be
very exciting and introduces an element of spontaneity when
you make your picture.

A mosaic collage

Create a mosaic collage, using small squares cut out from your coloured paper. Try to keep the squares roughly the same size to make the design simpler to arrange, without too many gaps. As you become more confident you can experiment with varying the sizes to add more interest to the picture. Plan out the image you want in advance by sketching your design on cartridge paper. Arranging and sorting the colours into a pattern or image can be extremely calming and absorbing. Experiment with accent colours and harmonies and see how you can use them to express a variety of emotions and moods.

Birds in Flight

Using shapes with calming watercolour

Working with a limited palette can be surprisingly rewarding as well as calming. It means that you don't need to make any more key decisions once you have selected your colour pairing. You can choose two harmonious colours such as yellow and blue, as I have done in this exercise, or refer back to the colour wheel on page 34 and opt for complementary colours such as yellow and purple. If you want to achieve a brighter result try using reds and oranges, which will give a hotter, more vibrant painting. The process of methodically building up the layers of paint, allowing the motifs to appear as if by magic, is extremely absorbing, and once you have established a rhythm the developing results can be exciting and surprising. You can adapt this process to all kinds of images and experiment with a variety of colour combinations, so I have included another example using a flower motif.

Be patient between stages as the paper must be completely dry before you move on. You could try working on a similar exercise during your waiting periods. This will also give you the chance to perfect your technique.

Therapeutic benefits

- Beautiful result suggesting movement and light through colour and motif
- Easy-to-do stages which require no drawing or colour mixing skills
- Builds confidence in watercolour painting technique
- Satisfaction in extending your range of skills by experimenting with glazing and washes.

Materials

23 x 31cm (9 x 12¼in) sheet
of 640gsm (300lb) NOT
watercolour paper

HB pencil

Soft or plastic eraser

Large wash brush

No. 10 and No. 2 round
watercolour brushes

Tissue

Watercolour paints

 Raw Sienna

Winsor Blue (Green
Shade)

| Prepare your paper by wetting it all over with clean water using the big wash brush. Drop in three brushloads of dilute Raw Sienna and three of Winsor Blue, letting the two colours mingle on the paper. Allow the water to do the painting and avoid disturbing the paint while it dries. Aim to achieve a pale, watery result.

When the paper is completely dry, draw the outline of a bird in pencil, erasing and correcting any mistakes as you go. You can copy the template above, but enlarge your bird to match those on pages 46–7. Position it on the paper towards the top right-hand corner.

2 Prepare a pool of dilute Raw Sienna and another of Winsor Blue. The colours will need to be a little stronger than the original mixes as they will dry lighter. Thoroughly wet the paper, first using the wash brush to apply clean water to the large areas, and then using the No. 10 brush to bring the water up to the outlines of the bird. Immerse the No. 10 brush in the pool of Raw Sienna so that the paint will drip a little when you lift it out. Lay the colour-loaded brush on the paper and allow the colour to run and spread. Do this a couple of times with Raw Sienna and then repeat with Winsor Blue. The colours will mingle with each other and run up to the edge of the bird. Then use the No. 2 brush to encourage the paint to come up neatly to the outlines, keeping the edges tidy and sharp.

The paper should remain wet throughout this stage. This will help you to achieve a soft, blended result. If beads of water and colour form at the edge of the paper, gently mop them up with a tissue or a slightly damp brush. Continue to mop up the beads until the shine starts to disappear because only then will the paint remain more or less where it is.

3 Wait again until the picture is completely dry and then draw two more bird silhouettes, tucking them slightly behind the first one to make a total of three birds. You may find it useful to make a template of the first bird using a tracing from the original and transferring it to a thicker piece of paper or thin card and cutting it out. You can then use this to draw round throughout the rest of the painting. Think carefully about how the new images relate to the first bird. The first will be a complete image and it will overlap any subsequent birds. In my example all the birds fly in one direction, but you can turn them round to give a different feeling of movement in the composition.

4 Keeping the three birds dry, repeat the wetting and dropping-in process using the same two colours. It's up to you where you put the colours. Glazing one over the other will create new colours in the picture. Interesting greens could start to emerge throughout this process. Work carefully around the birds, keeping the edges as neat as possible. Treat any spaces between the birds in the same way – dampen the area, however narrow, and add drops of colour using the No. 2 brush.

5 When the paper is completely dry,
use your template to draw two
more birds to make five. They will be
overlapped by the existing three birds so
will not have complete outlines.

6 Wet the paper thoroughly up to the
outlines of the five birds. You may
find it more challenging to keep the
paper wet throughout but you can help
this by adding plenty of water to the
larger areas. Add the colours as before,
but apply more Winsor Blue than Raw
Sienna and apply slightly stronger mixes
to the edges of the birds, allowing the
colour to run and blend. Treat the
small shapes as before by applying
water and dropping in colour with
the No. 2 brush.

7 Draw another two birds to make a total of seven, placing them at the back of the small flock.

8 Wet the paper thoroughly up to the outlines of the seven birds and add the colour around the outlines and smaller shapes. Use Raw Sienna on any remaining light areas, but otherwise use Winsor Blue throughout. When dry, draw two more birds to make a final total of nine.

9 Wet the paper again and apply Winsor Blue to the
edges of the birds, letting the colour flow and blend
into the water. When the blue is dry there may be smudges
where the paint has bled into the body of the bird, in which
case use a small, stiff, slightly damp brush to tease the paint
out and neaten the edges. Try to work delicately and clean
your brush regularly. Have some tissue handy to blot any
unwanted colour off the birds. Finally, give each bird an
'eye' using dilute Winsor Blue with the No. 2 brush. Stand
back and admire the result. You will be surprised how bright
the first bird appears against the surrounding, progressively
darker birds.

Alternative composition: Calming flowers

With the exception of the colours, the materials and processes in this exercise are the same as in the birds composition, using layers of coloured glazes to create a series of progressively darker images. As before, I have chosen relaxing, harmonious colours, this time pink, violet and blue.

Watercolour paints

 Permanent Rose

 French Ultramarine Blue

 Winsor Violet

 Quinacridone Gold

Still Life in Pen

Discover the clean, cool lines of penwork

At first, pen and line can seem to be a daunting medium because every mark you make is permanent, but you will soon learn to turn this to your advantage. With a little advance planning and practice you should find this a fairly easy exercise, though you will be surprised and rewarded by how professional the result can look.

Historically, artists used a pen and metal nib which, like a quill or feather pen, was dipped into a bottle of ink. The advantage of using this traditional technique is that marks can be varied and expressive. However, the main drawback is that the nibs are prone to create unwanted ink blots on your work. The need to constantly recharge the pen with ink can also interrupt the flow of your line work and your concentration.

For this reason I opt for the slightly more technical, prefilled 'fineliner' drawing pens which ensure a steady ink flow. Other obvious advantages are that the pens are low maintenance, and the ink is quick-drying and doesn't need replenishing. Drawing pens are also very portable, making them ideal for drawing outdoors; you can keep a pen and small sketchbook in your pocket and start drawing whenever and wherever you feel the urge.

This project begins with a few exercises to help you decide which angle of line suits you best. In the main stage-by-stage exercise you will use the pen to create a three-dimensional still-life drawing, while at the end you will find an alternative option that uses cross-hatching to give a more abstract result.

Therapeutic benefits

- The level of concentration required for this exercise should help you set aside everyday concerns
- Rhythmic movement in drawing the hatching can be very relaxing
- Initial drawing in pencil shows the benefits of planning in advance
- Impressive, positive results may surprise you
- Skills learned here are easily transferable to other drawing projects
- Quick and easy set-up introduces a medium ideal for impromptu artwork.

Materials

A3 sheet of 200gsm (120lb)
cartridge paper

HB pencil

Soft or plastic eraser

0.3mm and 0.5mm drawing pens

Hatching practice

Hatching is drawing parallel lines in one direction to create a range of tones determined by their density; the closer the lines are to each other the darker the tone will appear. Cross-hatched lines are similarly parallel but with another layer of hatching drawn on top, usually at right angles to the first. Do not be tempted to use a ruler for the hatched lines as it will give a hard, technical finish which will lack character.

As with all the exercises, you will benefit from spending a little time 'warming up'. This can be done by drawing trial sets of lines at different angles. You have the choice of diagonal left to right or diagonal right to left, or horizontal or vertical. Try them all out and see which seems to suit you best. I am left-handed and prefer right to left diagonal as it feels more comfortable. This is something you can practise to build up your confidence with the medium.

The subject matter for this exercise came from items that I have in my kitchen, showing that you can draw anything you have at hand. I arranged them in a classic triangular set-up, with the larger objects at the back and the smaller ones in the foreground.

As you can't make any changes after the ink is on the paper, it is best to start by making a pencil sketch of the still life (I have used pen here for clarity). Draw in all the information you need, including the edges of the shadows cast by the objects on the table surface. All the pencil lines will be erased once the pen work is complete, so don't worry if they are numerous.

2 Next, hatch in the main areas of shadow, including the shaded background
to highlight the objects. Make sure that your lines stop neatly at the pencil
contours; do not be tempted to add an outline as a boundary. You will find that
recognisable shapes begin to emerge as the hatching silhouettes the shape in front.
You can start off hatching in pencil if you are apprehensive, but soon you will
become more confident working directly with the pen. Keep the lines as neat as
possible but don't worry if there is the odd wobble or two! The pencil lines now
look very faint under the ink, but I left them in place as I prefer to save the erasing
for one go when the picture is completed.

3 Having drawn in the first layer of tone, you then need to add another layer of
hatching to create deeper shade and more depth in the picture. Put in more
hatching at the bottom of the egg, and also in the area of cast shadow where it
meets the egg. Add tone on the mug, vase and egg cup behind the eggs. This will
highlight the light on the eggs and the rims of the china objects. Finally, add more
hatching in the background, directly behind the objects. You will find the contrast
between light and dark areas increases as your lines become denser.

4 In the final stage you should build up the hatching to create even deeper tones. In places the lines will almost merge together and appear nearly black. The deeper you go with the darks the brighter the lights will seem. Try to keep the edges as neat as possible, but remember that outlines are not allowed! As the drawing develops you will realise that outlines are not necessary to make a drawing look complete – in fact they can appear to flatten out an object, giving an artificial, cartoon-like result.

When you are satisfied with your drawing, erase all the pencil marks. This will not only tidy up the image but introduce a lovely freshness to the finished work.

Alternative approach

In this exercise you can combine hatching with cross-hatching yet keep the
pen work to a minimum. This results in a flatter, more abstract, contemporary-
looking drawing. In the absence of an outline separating the eggs and the mug or
background, the hatching encourages the eye to finish off the image – a definite
example of less is more!

Dandelion Clocks

Decorative watercolour painting

Dandelion 'clocks' – round fluffy clusters of seeds that disperse when you blow them – remind us of summer days in childhood. The dandelion clock provides a fantastic opportunity to practise handling masking fluid and to use it in an expressive manner. This exercise may take some time and will benefit from your full concentration when using the masking fluid, but once you develop your own strategy it can become all-absorbing.

Masking fluid should be regarded like painting rather than 'blocking out' – it's a positive rather than negative process, so can require a little lateral thinking. If it's seen as a negative, blanking-out process, the results can be unsatisfactory. It often seems surprising that such a small change of mindset can make all the difference to the outcome – a useful lesson perhaps for many other everyday situations!

Refer to the colour wheel on page 34 and choose your own combinations – you don't need to follow the ones I've selected here. Experiment with creating different effects and moods. Harmonious colours next to one another on the colour wheel will create a gentler result, but if you want a more dynamic effect then choose opposite colours.

Therapeutic benefits

- Easy, confidence-building watercolour exercise
- Subject reminds us of summer days and childhood games
- Boosts confidence in using masking fluid.

Materials

23 x 31cm (9 x 12¼in) sheet of 640gsm (300lb) NOT watercolour paper

HB pencil

Soft or plastic eraser

Pen and nib

Masking fluid

Masking fluid brush or palette knife

No. 12 and No. 2 round watercolour brushes

Tissues

Watercolour paints

 Quinacridone Gold

 Burnt Sienna

 Burnt Umber

 Shadow (or a mix of Winsor Violet and Burnt Umber)

Draw the overall dandelion clocks and stems in pencil, placing them slightly off-centre. My example is in pen to make the image clearer for you to copy accurately. Within the heads, draw three concentric circles on which you can arrange the seeds. These can be carefully erased once the seeds have been drawn in.

To draw the individual seeds, start off by drawing a large, flattened U-shape on one of your circles. Add another, less flat U-shape inside the first one, and then draw a central stalk through the middle, extending the line to the centre of the clock. Draw all the seed heads in the same way. Don't worry if your pencil lines seem too heavy as the masking fluid will remove them when you rub it off. Also draw in some floating seeds in the background, using the same method.

2 Dip the nib of your pen into the masking fluid and carefully mask out all the
  pencil marks, including the stems and floating seeds. Aim to stay true to your
drawing by working slowly and methodically. If you make a mistake, wait until the
masking fluid is dry, rub off the section that is wrong with your finger or an eraser
and reapply. Use the palette knife to splatter masking fluid on to the background to
add texture and interest. Leave the masking fluid to dry thoroughly.

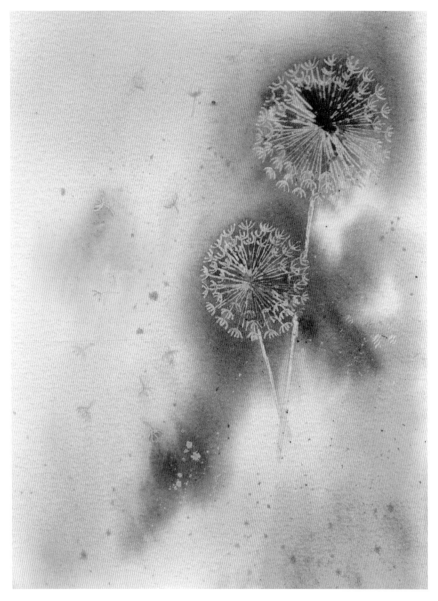

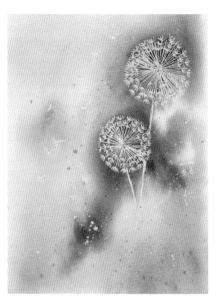

4 Once you are sure the paper is dry, remove all of the masking fluid by rubbing with a dry, clean finger and brush it away into a waste paper bin.

3 Prepare your paints by diluting them with clean water. Remember that the colours will be diluted by the water wash on the paper so they will need to be a bit stronger beforehand. The Shadow colour should be a little more concentrated as it will highlight the white seed heads. Wet the paper thoroughly all over with your wash brush – the paper should not dry before all the colours have been added as you will be aiming to achieve blended colours and there should be no hard edges. Apply the colours in the following order: Quinacridone Gold, Burnt Sienna and Shadow. Fill the No. 12 brush with paint and gently let it touch the paper so that the colours bloom and spread, mixing with the other colours. You can help them to spread by tickling the surface of the paper with your brush. The stronger Shadow mix will spread less. Try to retain some white areas between the shadow and the other colours.

Let the paint dry, keeping a watch for beads of water or colour developing around the edge of the paper. Lift them off the surface with a tissue to prevent any runbacks from spoiling the smooth finish of the wash of colours.

5 Use a little Burnt Umber to suggest the middle of the clocks, then mix it with Shadow to paint in
   some extra floating seeds in the background, using a No. 2 brush. A light splattering of colour in the
background adds to the texture. If any of the masking fluid splatters are too big and bright you can lightly
tint them with one of the background colours so they blend in with the overall picture.

Alternative compositions: Spider's web and lacy hogweed flowers

Spider's webs and the flowers of hogweed plants are also suited to this masking technique, but be careful to achieve the appropriate brush or pen marks for the subject. You can use fine lines and small dots to suggest a spider's web covered with water droplets and make small 'star' shapes in masking fluid to suggest the delicate hogweed flowers.

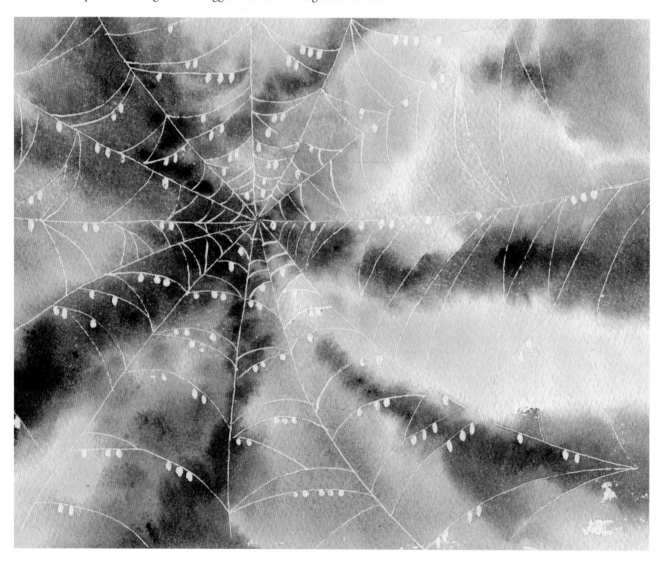

Having masked out the web, I thoroughly wet the paper and added brushloads of Indian Yellow, Green Gold and Payne's Grey, echoing the intricate radiating pattern created by the spider.

Here I have used Sap Green, French Ultramarine and Sepia to form a background suggestive of a grassy meadow and springtime sky. I wanted an almost abstract background that would highlight the fine detail of the hogweed.

Dotty Painting

Exploring Pointillism with acrylics

This Pointillist-inspired exercise requires a basic understanding of the colour wheel (see page 34). Pointillism is a technique developed in the late nineteenth century by some French Impressionist painters, using small dots of colour that together form an image. It is associated with the paintings of Georges Seurat and Paul Signac, who used their knowledge of the colour wheel to group colours so that from a distance they seem to blend together. You might wish to look at some of their paintings in a book or on the internet to discover how the basic elements of this project can be used at a more advanced level.

The Impressionists are credited with finding new colours in shadows, replacing black, grey and brown shadows with purples and blues, which add extra vibrancy to the work. So here you will use small brushstrokes of complementary colours, mingled with the main colours, to create shadows on and around the object you choose to paint.

The three exercises, showing an orange, a lemon and a sailing boat, are straightforward and enjoyable. Acrylic paints are an ideal medium for this project as they dry quickly, allowing you to work without the dots of colour running into each other. Using a large range of colours can help you achieve a brightness and spontaneity that can be lost if you have to spend time mixing your own colours, but if you do not have exactly the right colours try mixing and settle for a near compromise. It is not essential to completely cover the paper as any unpainted specks will add light and freshness to the final image. Place your brush in a water pot when it's not in use to prevent it drying out and permanently hardening the bristles. You can use watercolour paints instead, but you will need to wait longer for each layer of dots to dry.

Therapeutic benefits

- Bright and cheerful colours that are easy to use
- Fun and absorbing
- Easy paint application with small strokes all of the same size – so fewer decisions to make
- Enjoyment of painting natural objects
- Mistakes are easy to rectify using acrylics, so you can paint freely.

Materials

A3 sheet of 200gsm (120lb) cartridge paper

No. 0 round synthetic acrylic brush

HB pencil

Soft or plastic eraser

Acrylic paints

Titanium White

Ultramarine Blue

Alizarin Crimson

Cobalt Blue Hue

Deep Violet

Cadmium Orange Hue

Burnt Umber

Cadmium Yellow Hue

Yellow Ochre

Dotty orange

Fruit has been a feature of still life painting for centuries, but we shall give the subject a contemporary twist by using the Pointillist technique. Complementary colours, introduced on page 35, will be used to create shadows.

1 Draw the outline of the orange and its shadow in pencil. If it helps you to get started you can follow my example (drawn here in pen for clarity).

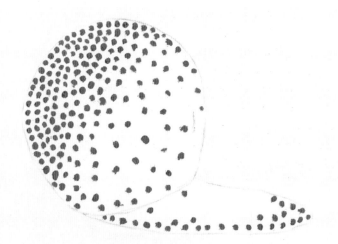

2 Mix the orange paint with a small amount of white and a little water to give the consistency of toothpaste. Apply closely packed dots of colour in the light, unshaded areas, and put a few dots in the shaded areas of both the orange and its shadow to give a hint of reflected colour and connect the orange and its shadow. Acrylic paint dries quickly, so you won't have to wait long before applying the next coloured dots.

3 Mix Cobalt Blue with a small amount of white and paint
  dots of this colour in the shaded area of the orange and
its shadow. Blue is opposite orange on the colour wheel and,
as you will have found in previous exercises, they boost each
other's strength, which enlivens the finished work. Allow
the dots to mingle in the spaces between the orange dots,
reducing the concentration as they move into the light area.
Mix a little white paint with Burnt Umber and Yellow Ochre
and place a few dots on the right-hand side to suggest where
the stalk was once attached.

4 Mix a little white paint with
  Cadmium Yellow Hue and paint
dots of this colour in the light areas
between the orange dots, allowing them
to become less concentrated in the
shadow area. Put a few dots of this mix
at the outer edge of the shadow.

5 Mix Deep Violet with a little white,
  and paint dots in the shaded area
and the shadow. Allow the dots to thin
out into the lighter areas of the orange.

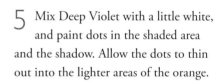

6 Add some pure, unmixed orange dots to the shaded side of the orange. Put in a few Alizarin Crimson dots in the shaded area and the shadow.

7 Finish off with a few Ultramarine Blue and Deep Violet dots in the darkest areas where the shaded part of the orange meets its shadow. After the paint is completely dry, erase any pencil lines that are still showing.

Materials

A3 sheet of 200gsm (120lb)
cartridge paper

No. 2 synthetic round acrylic
brush

HB pencil

Soft or plastic eraser

Acrylic paints

Titanium White

Yellow Ochre

Cadmium Yellow Hue

Burnt Umber

Cadmium Orange Hue

Phthalo Turquoise

Deep Violet

Dotty lemon

The second part of this exercise is to paint a lemon using the same technique as for
the orange. When you have mastered this you can continue to experiment with a
lime, an apple or your choice of any fruit or vegetable.

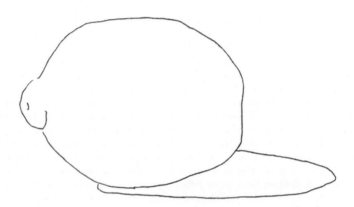

1 Draw the outline of the lemon and its shadow in pencil, just as with the orange.
If it helps you to get started you can follow my example (drawn here in pen
for clarity).

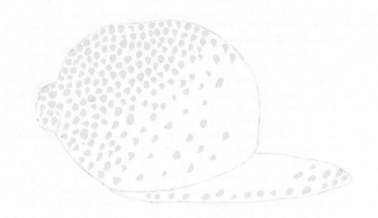

2 Mix Cadmium Yellow with a small amount of white and a little water to give
the consistency of toothpaste. Apply closely packed dots of colour in the light,
unshaded areas, and put a few dots in the shaded areas of both the lemon and its
shadow so as to give a hint of reflected colour and connect the two areas.

3 Mix Deep Violet with a small amount of white, and paint dots of this colour in the shaded area of the lemon and its shadow. Purple is opposite yellow on the colour wheel, so they increase each other's vibrancy. Allow the dots to mingle in the spaces between the yellow dots, reducing the concentration as they move into the light area. Mix a little white paint with Burnt Umber and Yellow Ochre and place a few dots on the left-hand side to suggest where the stalk was once attached.

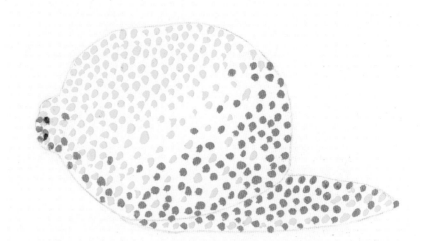

4 Using pure Cadmium Yellow, paint in dots of colour in the light areas between the light yellow dots, allowing them to become less concentrated in the shadow area. Put a few dots of this mix at the outer edge of the shadow.

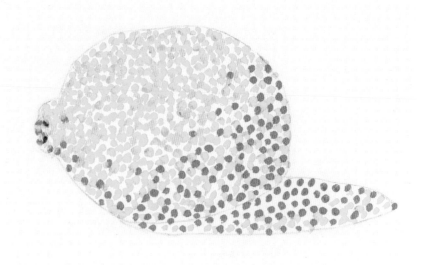

5 Mix the turquoise paint with a little
   white, and paint dots of this colour
in the shaded area of the lemon and its
shadow. Again allow the dots to thin
out into the lighter areas of the lemon.
Add some yellow mixed with white and
a very small amount of turquoise to give
a green-yellow, and put some dots in
the lighter areas.

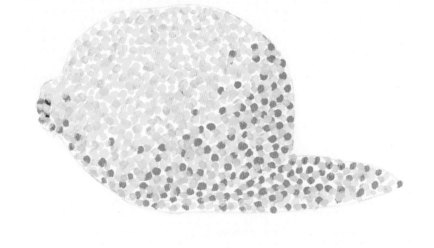

6 Mix the yellow with a little orange
   and place some dots on the shaded
side of the lemon. Add a few more to
the outer edge of the shadow. Finish off
with Deep Violet dots in the darkest
areas where the shadow of the lemon
meets the shadow cast by the lemon.
Finally, erase any pencil lines.

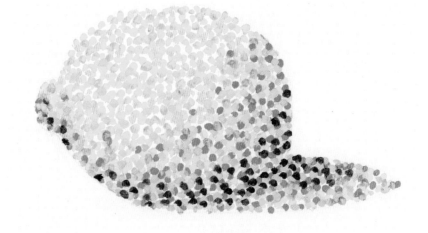

Materials

½ imperial (38 x 56cm/15 x 22in) 300gsm (140lb) NOT watercolour paper

HB pencil

No. 2 synthetic round acrylic brush

Soft or plastic eraser

Kitchen towel

Acrylic paints

Titanium White

Deep Violet

Ultramarine Blue

Cerulean Blue

Phthalo Blue

Cobalt Blue

Yellow Ochre

Sap Green

Cadmium Yellow Hue

Burnt Sienna

Cadmium Red Hue

Ivory Black

Dotty sailing boat

This final part of the Pointillist exercise shows how you can apply your new skills in a larger landscape composition. I have chosen a sailing boat on a breezy day that is reminiscent of George Seurat's outdoor scenes. The source photograph was taken at a sailing club in a beautiful nature reserve not far from my home. When it is sunny, it is a very special place to unwind and set aside daily worries and stresses! This picture is larger than some of the others in this book, so it will take you longer to complete. You don't have to paint it in one go, though – you can take time out for an hour or two here and there to add another layer of dots and dashes.

The three stages below show the beginning, middle and end of this exercise, but essentially it's just a case of building up marks and dots of colour to fill most of the paper. White flecks of paper between the coloured dots will contribute to the freshness of the scene. It doesn't matter if you don't have all the colours given here as you can mix a wide range by simply varying the amount of white paint that you add to the main colour. If you are mixing a light colour, start with white and add a little of the main colour, such as blue, in small increments to keep control over the mix. Keep some kitchen roll on hand to clean any excess paint off your brush before rinsing it in water.

Using an HB pencil, make a simple line drawing of the scene on your paper, following the drawing shown for guidance.

2 Plot out some of the main colours
   with dots of paint to establish
the key features in the picture, such
as the sail, sky, water and trees. Use
Cerulean Blue and Ultramarine Blue
straight from the tube in the sky and
water, followed by white with a dash
of Deep Violet in the sail, and white
with a little Phthalo Blue in the sky
and the water. Next, put in some white
and Cobalt Blue in the sky and water,
followed by Sap Green, Yellow Ochre,
Cadmium Yellow and Burnt Sienna
in the trees and island. To make the
darker greens, mix Sap Green with
Ultramarine Blue. Put Cadmium Red
accent colour dots on the triangle on
the sail. Add some white and Yellow
Ochre dots in the sail, and in the water
to start to suggest the reflection of the
boat. Blacks and greys are used only for
the sailor's clothing. Greys can be made
by gradually adding white to black
until the required shade is achieved.
Once all the main shapes of the
painting are in place, wait for the paint
to dry and erase any pencil guidelines.

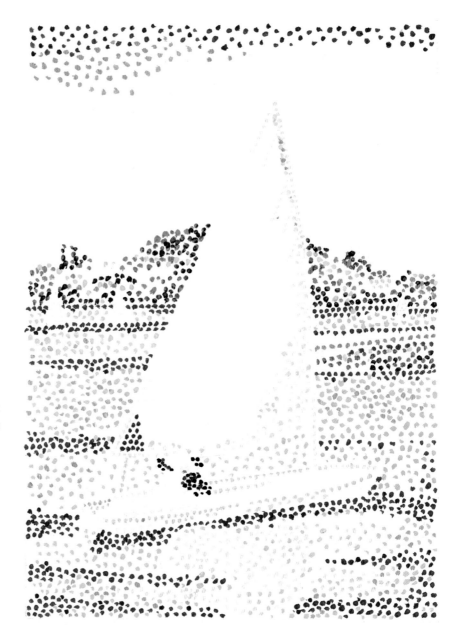

3 Gradually build up the coloured dots and dashes until you have more or less covered the whole paper. The brushstrokes can overlap in places, and you should aim to fill most of the gaps with colour. Some more subtly different colours, such as light Cobalt Blue, light Ultramarine Blue and light Cerulean Blue, can help to achieve a harmonious, blended result when you look at the painting from a distance, in much the same way that Seurat achieved. The optical effect of the dots and dashes seems to reinforce the overall impression of flickering light and movement.

Village Window

Warm hues in watercolour

take my camera whenever I go out so I can record potential images for paintings. Traditionally, artists are supposed to take a sketchbook everywhere, but I'm not always comfortable drawing in public – and after all, many Impressionist painters embraced the new photographic technology in the late nineteenth century.

I came across this window while wandering through a series of small villages in the Anti-Atlas Mountains in Morocco. The rich pink colours of the man-made walls can be found in the stunning rocks and mountainsides surrounding these villages. I thought this window would make an interesting subject as I was intrigued to know about the lives of the people behind the purple grille. Who lives there, how many rooms are there and how are they arranged? What jobs do the inhabitants have, does the dark interior offer respite from the sun in a hot country? Often the plainest external walls give no hint of the extraordinary richness of the interiors. The sense of mystery is very compelling and invites the viewer to speculate.

In this exercise you will be learning the importance of planning the painting process yet at the same time allowing for experimentation and unexpected results. The calm, soothing colours derive directly from the palette of the earth, and their natural harmony makes them a pleasure to handle.

Therapeutic benefits

- Easy, single subject
- Builds confidence with easy colour-mixing and application
- Brings memories of relaxing travel and summer holidays.

Materials

23 x 31cm (9 x 12¼in) sheet
of 640gsm (300lb) NOT
watercolour paper

HB pencil

Soft or plastic eraser

Palette knife or toothbrush

Pen and nib (medium size)

Large wash brush

No. 10 and No. 2 round
watercolour brushes

Masking fluid

Tissues

Watercolour paints

Raw Sienna

Burnt Sienna

Quinacridone Gold

Burnt Umber

Brown Madder

Indian Red

Shadow (or a mix of
Winsor Violet and
Burnt Umber)

1 Draw the window in
pencil, placing it to the
centre left of your page so
as to leave space for the
wall around. Concentrate
on getting the proportion
of the window right, and
the patterns of the grille,
but without aiming for
photographic accuracy.
Have your eraser to hand
just in case you make any
errors and need to redraw.

2 Then draw over the
metal grille with
masking fluid using a pen
and nib – you should
be able to achieve a very
fine line. I have used
pink masking fluid. With
a brush, mask out the
window frame and then,
after temporarily covering
the window area with a
piece of paper, splatter
some of the masking
fluid over the wall with
either a toothbrush or
a palette knife.

3 When the masking fluid is dry, use your wash brush to wet the paper thoroughly up to the masked-out window frame, then drop in brushstrokes of Raw Sienna and Quinacridone Gold with the No. 10 brush, aiming for an uneven effect. The colour strength should be a little stronger than you want for the final result as the mix will become further diluted by the clean water on the paper. As the wash dries you may find beads of water and colour forming at the edge of the picture. Mop these up immediately with tissue to avoid ugly run-backs.

4 When the wash is completely dry, thoroughly wet the wall area again and drop in more brushstrokes of slightly stronger Brown Madder and Indian Red. Mop up any pools of colour that may form at the edges of the paper as before. Let this dry. Using Shadow and Brown Madder, paint in the area behind the grille.

5 Let everything dry thoroughly and then remove all the masking fluid by rubbing it off with a dry finger.

6 Use a Raw Sienna and Burnt Sienna mix in various combinations to paint the window surround. Paint in all the purple-greys on the window frame and the pinky browns of the chipped stone. Tint the grille with light Shadow using a No. 2 brush, ensuring that some of the white remains. If any of your splattering on the wall looks too bright and prominent when the masking is removed, use the small brush to tint the dots with very watery versions of the browns you have been using.

7 Mix up a strong combination of Burnt Umber and Shadow, using plenty of paint. With clean water, carefully wet the picture, including the window surround but excluding the grille area. Drop in the strong mix at three points along the bottom edge of the window, and let it drip down in much the same way as rainwater would drip down a real wall. Tilt the picture to near vertical to encourage the drips (don't be tempted to put it flat until the shine has started to disappear, which indicates that the paint is drying). While the painting is still damp, lightly splatter the colours you have been using with a toothbrush or palette knife to add texture. The splatters can run a little to help embed them in the painting.

Landscape Collage

Making a collage from found material

In this exercise I have used pieces of paper torn from magazines, which can be a faster and more convenient alternative to painting your own collage paper – all you need do is look through some old magazines and use the colours in the pictures to make your own composition. Tearing the shapes out rather than using scissors adds another dimension to the end result; the softer, more painterly edges to the areas of colour give the image an organic, natural feel.

The process of tearing paper also encourages you to focus more on the shapes you are creating. Finer details are harder to achieve, which means that your final image will be a simplified version of the picture you are working from. Don't worry about achieving realistic detail as it's an overall impression you are aiming for, which can be quite liberating. The range of colours and tones in a magazine should give you plenty of options for creating blended effects and forms. I keep a folder in which I save magazine pages with good colour ranges for use in collages.

After you have mastered the basic collage techniques you could try using pages with various sizes of text to create interesting patterns and effects. You could also introduce alternative materials such as fabric samples, bus tickets, kitchen foil and even buttons and shells. The only stipulation is that they should adhere effectively to your base paper or board. In the early twentieth century, artists such as Georges Braque and Pablo Picasso famously combined collage with drawing and painting to great effect, so don't feel constrained if you want to follow their lead as you grow in confidence.

The landscape picture used here is an easy exercise to develop your collage skills further. You may like to begin by making a basic colour wheel from paper torn from magazines – a useful way to familiarise yourself with selecting, tearing and sticking printed material. Try to follow the sequence of colours in the example shown here.

Therapeutic benefits

- Sorting coloured papers and shapes is an enjoyable exercise
- The tactile process of tearing paper by hand can be absorbing
- Tearing rather than drawing shapes encourages you to look at shape and form in a different way
- Sticking coloured paper takes us back to childhood days.

Materials

A4 sheet of cartridge paper

HB pencil

Colour magazines

PVA glue

Glue spreader and an old plate (or similar)

Using an HB pencil, copy the landscape line drawing, sketching in the main features. Don't worry too much about detail as you will be covering this drawing with paper.

2 Find a selection of different yellows and arrange them on the paper in the 'cornfield' area. When you are satisfied, use the spreader to add a little glue to the back of each piece, and stick them down in turn. Do the same with some lighter blues for the lower areas of sky just above the horizon to reinforce depth and perspective. Try to use colours that are progressively lighter or darker to create a gently graded effect rather than an abrupt contrast of tone.

3 Put in darker purple-blues at the top of the sky. Stick down some yellows in the distant 'cornfield' and lay in some greens for the hill just above it. Put a line of light green at the bottom of the hedge in the foreground.

4 Find some more greens, both light and dark, and tear out shapes for the hedges and trees in the background. The thin green strips can be quite fiddly to achieve, but don't worry if you end up with shorter sections as these will suggest smaller clumps rather than a single, long hedge. Find a light brown and tear out a small square for the house, and a dark brown for the triangle of the roof. Carefully tear out some thin green pieces to suggest the poppy stems and then use reds and oranges to make the flowers. I used more thin green pieces to make the field pattern in the middle distance, and put some yellow shapes between them to accentuate the furrowed texture.

5   Brighten up the foreground by adding some more poppies. Red is opposite to
    green on the colour wheel and will act as an accent colour which will enliven
the picture. Finally, fill any gaps you may have with an appropriate colour, and
check that all your pieces are fully stuck to the paper.

Alternative composition: Jug collage

Still lifes can be just as effective as landscapes when using collage. For this jug, I
simply drew an outline in pencil and worked directly from observation, matching
the collage paper colours as well as I could.

Beautiful Butterflies

Using stained-glass colours in ink

The remarkable patterns that occur in the natural world are particularly apparent when you look closely at a butterfly. In this exercise we shall examine the stunning design of a butterfly wing and use coloured ink to render a simplified, abstract version of the real thing. The vibrant colours of the inks give a sense of transparency to the delicate wing, while the black outlines give the overall image a look not unlike stained glass. I drew the butterfly images from photographs and simplified them by picking out the overall patterns and colours rather than being too precise. The simplicity of the images and the bright colours lend themselves well to the vivid selection of inks available. Try doing this exercise in watercolours to see the difference.

This is an easy exercise as the colour is taken directly from the bottle with no mixing or dilution in order to achieve maximum freshness and glow. Although the selected colours are not completely true to nature they work well together and the image will be a cheerful and lively one. A steady hand and patience are helpful in achieving the clear outlines; I rest my hand firmly on the work surface to keep a steady control of the brush. Use a good brush with a fine point and keep on dipping it in the ink so it flows well. Small errors can be absorbed into the black ink but any bigger ones cannot be covered over, so set aside enough time to do this exercise and avoid distractions.

You can use the same original drawing over and over again, applying different colours on the wings but retaining black for the outlines. Repeating it at different angles on a large sheet of paper will give you interesting patterns. To do this, make your original drawing on cartridge paper then place a sheet of transfer paper between that and the sheet of watercolour paper for your finished artwork. Simply outline the original drawing with a pencil, and your lines will be transferred on to your watercolour paper. I often use red transfer paper to distinguish the marks from pencil. If you prefer, a single image drawn directly on the final watercolour paper could form the centrepiece of a greeting card or one-off painting.

I used a bright white watercolour paper (Saunders Waterford High White) to make the most of the vibrant ink colours. It is possible to work on a heavy cartridge paper (no less than 200gsm/120lb), but the extra absorbency can make the finish less even. Watercolour paper allows a longer drying time so the ink will flow more freely. By keeping the drawing simple, you can achieve a flat, abstract effect which accentuates the pattern and symmetry of the wings.

Therapeutic benefits

- The chance to look closely at patterns in the natural world
- Easy-to-use colours with confidence-boosting results
- Satisfying exercise that can be managed in easy steps reasonably quickly
- Adding your artwork to cards is a rewarding way to share your achievements with friends and family - the simple images in vibrant colours are also great for sharing on social media.

Orange butterfly

Butterflies are synonymous with warm summer months when flowers are in bloom. In this exercise we shall capture their bright colours and striking patterns that we normally only see in a fleeting glimpse.

Materials

A3 sheet of 300gsm (140lb) NOT watercolour paper

HB pencil

Soft or plastic eraser

Cartridge paper (optional)

Transfer paper (optional)

No. 6 and No. 2 round watercolour brushes

0.1mm water-resistant fineliner drawing pen

Drawing Inks

Winsor & Newton range

Canary Yellow

Orange

Deep Red

Nut Brown

Blue

Emerald

Black

1   Draw the butterfly carefully in pencil (my first example here is drawn in pen for clarity), correcting any mistakes with your eraser. If you want to keep your initial drawing for repeat images, draw the image on cartridge paper, then use transfer paper to copy the image on to the watercolour paper. The outlines will merge with the inks and largely disappear during the painting process. If you only want a one-off image, draw directly on to the watercolour paper in pencil.

2   Paint in the red ink at the top of the wings, followed by orange and yellow. Use the No. 6 brush for the larger areas and the No. 2 for the fiddly sections. Leave any white areas unpainted as the paper is bright enough.

3 With the No. 2 brush, paint the small blue specks, the blue rings around some of the white areas, the green on the body and head, and the brown on the head and sides of the body. Using the tip of your brush, carefully paint the antennae in blue – I recommend practising this first on a spare sheet of paper.

4 Finish off the butterfly by painting all the black areas using the No. 6 brush for larger areas and the No. 2 for the details. A fine black line around the outer edge of the white spots and antennae will add the finishing touches. Details such as this can be more easily done with a 0.1mm fineliner drawing pen than a brush.

Materials

A3 sheet of 300gsm (140lb) NOT watercolour paper

HB pencil

Soft or plastic eraser

Cartridge paper (optional)

Transfer paper (optional)

No. 6 and No. 2 round watercolour brushes

0.1mm water-resistant fineliner drawing pen

Drawing Inks

Winsor & Newton range

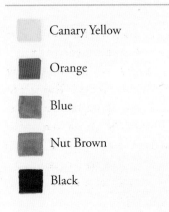

Canary Yellow

Orange

Blue

Nut Brown

Black

Brown butterfly

This exercise is similar to the orange butterfly but develops your skills further. The main differences are a softer range of colour and the use of a glazing technique to overlay the ink in some areas to achieve a subtle colour change. Otherwise the overall effect is essentially the same, with a simplified, stained-glass effect which accentuates the brilliance of the coloured ink.

Make a pencil drawing directly on to the watercolour paper, copying my example and using your eraser to correct any mistakes. Alternatively, if you want to repeat your image, make the original drawing on cartridge paper then use transfer paper as in the Orange butterfly exercise (see page 92).

2 Use the No. 6 brush to paint in the yellow areas on the wings and body. Change to the No. 2 brush to paint the three orange areas and the blue stripes. Add the small spot on the large wing, the eye and the leg.

3 Dilute some of the brown ink with a few drops of water on a small plate or palette. Use this to 'glaze' over some of the yellow area. Glazing is the term for applying a light, transparent wash over another colour to modify it – in this instance, it will darken the yellow areas. Keeping the glaze very dilute will allow the original colour to shine through.

4 Next, paint in the brown areas using undiluted ink. Nut Brown is a much more muted colour so it doesn't have the intensity of some of the brighter colours such as red and orange.

5 Lastly, paint in the black areas, using the No. 6 brush for the larger areas and the No. 2 for detail. The drawing pen will give greater accuracy for making the very fine lines and adding speckles on the wings and body.

Butterfly composition

The final example shows how you can make a composition using the two butterflies. I drew both then added some grass blades in the same simplified style. I painted the butterflies using the stages described on pages 92–6 and added colour to the grass, using Emerald Green and Viridian (you can add a little Blue to the Emerald Green if you don't have Viridian). I didn't want a strong background, so I diluted Blue with plenty of water, mixing well. After I had painted the background with this mix, I finished by adding some black lines around and on the leaves with a No. 2 brush.

Patterns with Cling Film

An abstract composition in watercolour

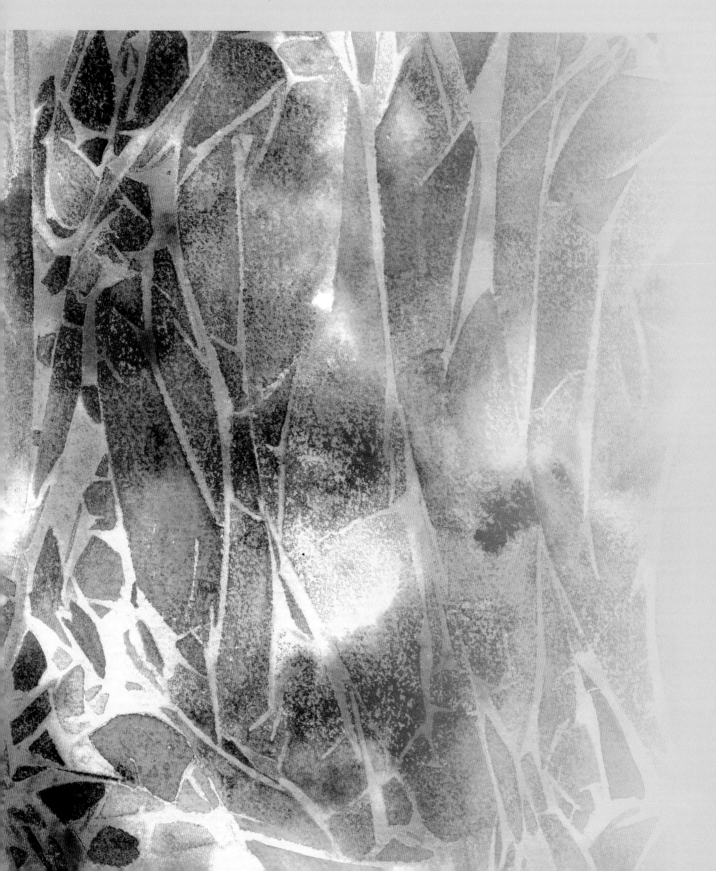

It can be very exciting to start a painting without knowing what the end result will look like. This is a straightforward yet very absorbing exercise that requires neither particular drawing skills nor experience of mixing colours. Instead, you will simply choose colours which then form abstract shapes that will be your artwork. An abstract composition uses shape, form, colour and line as its subject matter, rather than depicting recognisable features. This exercise will give you an insight into the thought processes involved when making an abstract work.

There are skills, too, that you will pick up during the exercise. You will learn about opaque and transparent colours, which paints stain and which ones 'granulate'. Watercolour paints can range from transparent to opaque, and this is usually indicated on the tube label – a white square means that the paint is transparent, a square with a diagonal line means the paint is semi-transparent. A solid black square means the paint is opaque, and a black triangle indicates semi-opaque. These differences can be significant when you are using watercolours. Transparent and semi-transparent paints are perfect for glazes (a light wash laid on top of a dry wash, which creates a new colour), whereas opaque colours simply cover the underpainting. I generally try to avoid using fully opaque colours as they can appear heavy and dominate a painting.

Another useful piece of information on the tube label tells you if the paint stains, indicated by the code 'st'. This means that the pigment becomes fixed and usually won't be disturbed if you place a glaze on top. Granulating paints, indicated by a 'g' on the label, give a textured appearance on the paper, and when they are mixed or glazed with others you can achieve some lovely results. This type of paint is particularly suited to cloudy skies. While you are working it can be helpful to keep a note of these various characteristics so you become more familiar with the effects they create. If you use pans rather than tubes you may not have all this information readily available, but it can be found on the manufacturer's website.

In this exercise you will also develop your brush skills, using a No. 6 for larger areas and No. 2 for the smaller details. Gaining confidence with finer brushwork will be helpful in all your painting.

One particularly enjoyable aspect of this exercise is using cling film to generate random abstract shapes. You will find the physical act of gently moving the cling film around on the paper with your fingers is fun as you watch patterns emerging on the paper. Creating textures with cling film in this way can also be useful in future projects to suggest tree bark, mountains or moving water.

Therapeutic benefits

- Extremely absorbing and physically engaging
- Encourages flexibility, because you are responding to a randomly created starting point
- There is no right or wrong - you can allow your imagination to take over
- Learn new skills without trying too hard
- Achieve dramatic, interesting and unexpected results.

Materials

23 x 31cm (9 x 12¼in) sheet of 640gsm (300lb) NOT watercolour paper

Large wash brush

No. 10, No. 6 and No. 2 round watercolour brushes

Cling film

Watercolour paints

Yellow Ochre

Winsor Blue (Green Shade)

Brown Madder

Sepia

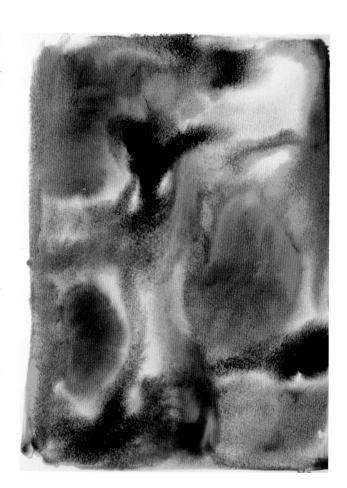

As you will need to apply a layer of cling film to wet paint, the first part of this exercise needs to be done quickly, so gather together all the materials before you start. You will need a sheet of cling film slightly bigger than your sheet of paper.

Prepare your paints first. Loosen all four colours with some water using the No. 10 brush. The paint should be fairly strong as it will become diluted as soon as it touches the dampened paper. Using the wash brush and clean water, wet the paper thoroughly all over. Apply three No. 10 brushloads of each colour to the paper, working from light to dark – Yellow Ochre, Brown Madder, Winsor Blue and lastly Sepia. The colours should 'bloom' and run into one another. Don't worry about any puddles of colour that occur, nor about tidying up the edges.

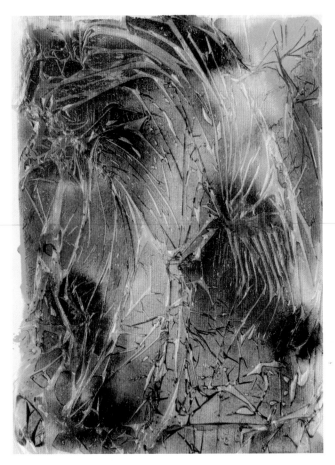

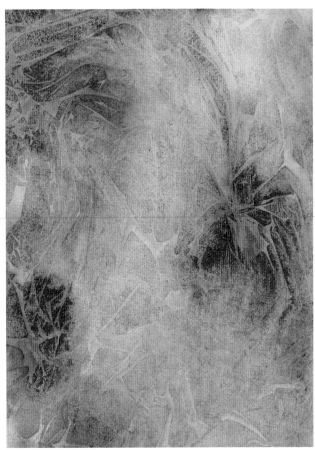

2 Lay the cling film loosely over the wet paint. Press it
down firmly, but at the same time encouraging creases
to form. These will make angular shapes appear in the paint
underneath. Any large air pockets that remain can be gently
pushed to the edge of the paper with your fingers. You will see
interesting patterns developing under the cling film, and these
will form the main features of your abstract composition.

3 Wait until the paper is completely dry before moving the
cling film. This can take up to 30 minutes, but don't be
tempted to speed this up by using a hairdryer as it could blow
away your cling film.

4 Carefully lift a corner of the cling film and check that the paint underneath is dry. If it is, peel away all the cling film and examine the patterns that have been formed – if it's still even a little wet, leave it for another 10 minutes. Next, with the No. 6 and No. 2 brushes and the four colours you used for the initial washes, paint over some of the shapes you find between the light lines. Choose colours that are different from those underneath, and keep the paint fairly transparent to allow the base colour to show through.

5 Now you can add to your painting. Simply continue to follow your instincts and paint in
   as many or as few shapes as you want, letting your imagination take over. You will see an
interesting composition emerge that will suggest movement and light. You may find that some
of the shapes suggest birds or fish, for example, in which case you can choose to reinforce this
by adding features such as an eye or a fin, shifting the picture away from an abstract.

   This exercise can be easily repeated using a different combination of colours, and the beauty
of it is that it will always produce a different result.

Watercolour paints

- Burnt Sienna

- Green Gold

- Indian Yellow

- Viridian

- Winsor Blue (Green Shade)

Alternative compositions

In this example I applied the colours as before, allowing them to bloom on the paper. I then placed the cling film on top while the paint was still wet and let the paper dry. I used the shapes created by the cling film to provide the basis of the painting. In this case I found that I could build up several layers of rich colour and decided to fill the paper more than in the first example. With its broad range of greens and yellows, the result reminds me of leaves and foliage.

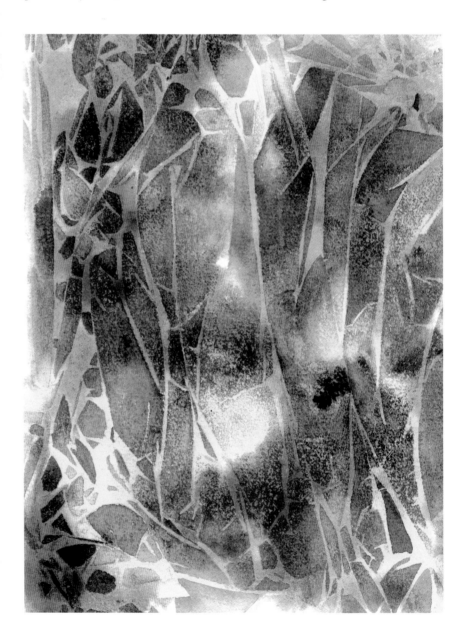

Watercolour paints

Cerulean Blue

Winsor Blue (Green Shade)

Cobalt Blue

Payne's Grey

This example shows how you can create a very different feel to your composition by using an alternative range of colours. The blues here remind me of icy water and have a cool feeling. You can use cling film to suggest patterns in ice if you are painting a snow scene. I left some areas untouched when I felt the painting was complete – there is no need to paint over the entire picture.

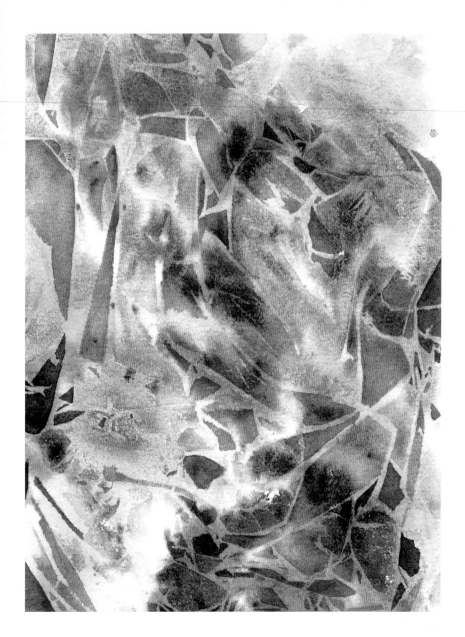

Field of Tulips

A perspective exercise using pastel pencils

This exercise uses simple one-point perspective to create depth and distance in your pictures. You will probably be familiar with images of railway tracks that seem to converge at the distant horizon. Anything else that is parallel to the tracks, such as a verge or fence, will also seem to meet at the same 'vanishing point' on the horizon. Features that are in reality identical in size will appear to become smaller as they near the vanishing point – for example, the wooden railway sleepers become progressively narrower in the distance.

The simplified version of tulip fields that follows shows how these principles apply in a different context. This exercise will focus not only on applying the principles of one-point perspective, but also on the patterns created by the lines of tulips. Holland's tulip fields are understandably a very popular springtime tourist destination and the stripes of bright, cheerful colours make them an ideal subject for artists.

I used pastel pencils for this exercise as they give a wide choice of bright colours and are easier to apply than coloured pencils, though the latter would be a good second choice. Pastel pencils are enjoyable to work with and their softness makes them simple to blend, adding greater depth to your colours. Because you will be working on a large sheet of paper in this exercise, they are ideal as they allow you to cover the paper easily but also draw in finer details than bigger, soft pastels would allow. The colours here are from Derwent's Pastel Pencils set of 36 colours; other manufacturers may use different names for the colours, but you should be able to find a close match. If need be you can mix the colours, and there's nothing wrong with some compromises here and there.

Finally, when your picture is complete, spray it with fixative or hairspray to prevent the pastel from smudging. Ideally, use two or three light layers sprayed from a distance of about 30cm (12in), allowing each to dry before applying the next – a single, dense spray at close distance can add unwanted textures, and at worst dissolve the pastel. Even fixed pastels can smudge, so when storing your work, place some tissue paper or newsprint on top to prevent the colour transferring to other pieces of work.

Therapeutic benefits

- Bright, cheerful colours
- Tulips evoke memories of springtime, the season of growth and rebirth
- Mastering perspective techniques increases your artistic confidence
- Easy-to-apply colours, using gentle, rhythmic strokes
- Dramatic, accomplished results that will impress family and friends.

Pastel Pencils

Derwent range

- Cerulean Blue
- French Grey Light
- Prussian Blue
- Forest Green
- Spectrum Orange
- Raspberry
- Violet
- Magenta
- Vanilla
- Sepia
- May Green
- Pea Green
- Ionian Green
- Green Oxide
- Naples Yellow
- Cadmium Red
- Dioxazine Purple
- Flesh
- Process Yellow
- Dark Sanguine
- Titanium White

Materials

A2 sheet of 200gsm (120lb) cartridge paper

HB pencil

Ruler

Soft or plastic eraser

Cotton buds

Artist's fixative or hairspray

Perspective practice

For this practice exercise, use an A4 sheet of cartridge paper. Following the example provided, make a pencil drawing of the railway tracks, trees and bushes. Note how all these elements converge on the horizon line at a single 'vanishing point'. The sleepers and landscape elements will gradually decrease in width and height as they converge towards the vanishing point. It is surprising how easily the illusion of depth can be given through line alone.

Start the main exercise by scaling up the template drawing shown of the tulip field by a factor of three on the A2 sheet of cartridge paper. To do this, draw a rectangular frame measuring 30cm x 43.5cm (11¾ x 17in). Then measure the template from the top edge to the horizon line (ignoring the trees and houses), multiply this by three and make a mark at this distance down from the top of the frame on both sides. Next, the points on the bottom frame: measure their distance from the sides, multiply each by three, and mark the scaled-up positions along the bottom frame on the A2 sheet. Repeat this process along the two vertical edges where any significant lines touch the frame. Next, measure the distance from the left edge of the frame on the template to the left side of the base of the windmill. Multiply this by three and mark it on the horizon line on your main drawing. Then measure, multiply and mark the width of the windmill itself. Measure from the top of the frame to the top of the windmill (excluding the sails), and plot this in. Draw in the low wall at the bottom of the windmill and mark the vanishing point at the centre of the top of this wall. Using a pencil and ruler, lightly join up each mark you have made at the frame edges with the vanishing point to achieve a fan-like effect.

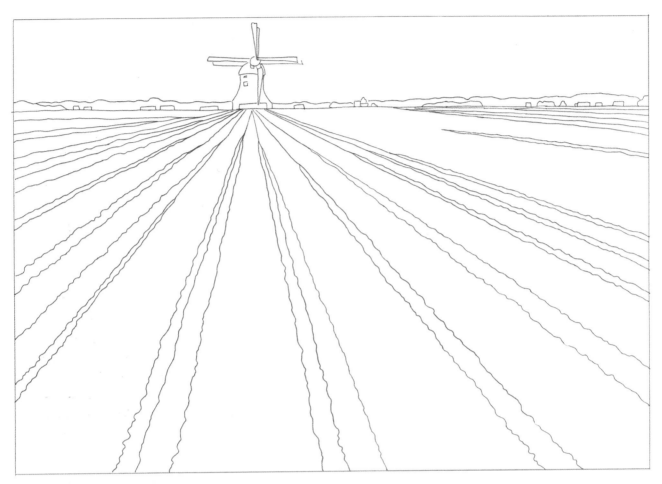

2 You will now have marked in the overall position of the windmill, so draw in the detail (you may be surprised how small it appears). Draw in the outlines of the distant mountains, trees and houses on the horizon, either by measuring or by eye, but be careful not to make them too big. Next, referring to the example, draw over your ruled lines by hand to make them look more natural. Erase any ruled lines that still show.

3 Now you are ready to add an initial layer of colour. Lightly shade the main areas of colour with the pastels. Aim to lightly cover each area before you add detail. Use Cerulean Blue for the sky, Prussian Blue for the distant hills and Forest Green for the trees. The windmill is mainly Sepia with a little Dark Sanguine on the right side and French Grey Light on the windows. The houses are Titanium White. Colour the tulips, working around the 'fan' shape in an anti-clockwise direction. The sequence of colours (starting from the left side under the horizon) is: Spectrum Orange, Ionian Green, May Green, Violet, Process Yellow, Magenta, Process Yellow, Pea Green, Dioxazine Purple, Pea Green, Cadmium Red, Pea Green, Magenta, May Green, Flesh, Vanilla, Pea Green, Process Yellow, Vanilla, Green Oxide, Raspberry, Green Oxide, Process Yellow, Green Oxide, Spectrum Orange, Green Oxide, Process Yellow, Green Oxide, Violet, Green Oxide, Process Yellow, Ionian Green, Spectrum Orange, Magenta, Violet, Cadmium Red and Naples Yellow.

4 The next step is to build up all of the colours with extra layers, mixing where needed, to increase their intensity. For example, add a layer of Cadmium Red over the Raspberry to brighten it up and create more depth. Put another layer of Cerulean Blue in the sky, followed by a layer of Titanium White so it mixes to a lighter blue. The earth furrows in the foreground are Vanilla, but with an added layer of Naples Yellow to give a deeper colour. Add Process Yellow into the distant first stripe of May Green, on the left side just below the horizon line, to make a more vivid lime green. The picture should start to look much more intense and vibrant. Using either a cotton bud or your finger, gently rub over the colours, blending them to eliminate any remaining white areas of the paper. Keep your fingers clean (or use new cotton buds) to prevent contaminating areas with unwanted colour.

5 Continue to build up the colours, adding shadows where necessary to suggest depth. Add some Forest Green to the sides of the green stripes in the foreground and some thin lines of the same colour to break up the large yellow area on the right. Deepen the colours on the horizon using the original colours, and add some Sepia and Flesh to the blades of the windmill. Put in a small amount of Dark Sanguine to suggest roofs on the distant houses along the horizon. You can also put a little Dark Sanguine at the sides of the Vanilla/Naples Yellow stripes for shadow. When you have finished, gently spray your picture with fixative, then stand back and admire your work.

Upside-down Portrait

A challenging exercise in pencil

Our familiarity with the human face makes the portrait one of the most difficult subjects for an artist – we think we know what we can see, but we don't really look. Some artists find portraiture so engaging that they dedicate their whole artistic career to the subject, whereas others avoid it completely. A good portrait will give the viewer an insight into the character of the sitter, and if you choose to draw someone you know well, you may find that your familiarity with them is helpful. However, it may even be a hindrance to your work as you may not be able to view them subjectively.

In many years of teaching students to draw portraits, I have found that a good way for them to gain initial confidence is to work from a photograph – the image is already translated into two dimensions, and it's less intimidating than looking closely at a real face. In this exercise, you will also turn the original photo upside down, and draw your picture upside down too. This is a little like drawing abstract shapes, which makes it easier to follow what you actually see rather than what your brain thinks you should see.

By following the stages in this exercise you'll be able to produce a drawing that will be more effective than you might expect. The main rule is to work upside down throughout – no peeping, however tempted you are to check your progress halfway through. You'll use pencils of different hardness. H pencils are harder than B pencils, and the greater the number, the harder or softer they become respectively (see also page 8). HB is in the middle, so is a good all-round choice.

Pencil grades

6H

4H

2H

HB

2B

4B

6B

Therapeutic benefits

- Offers a very impressive and rewarding result
- Encourages 'lateral thinking' - looking at a problem in a different way
- Builds confidence - you will be surprised at what you can achieve
- Drawing portraits encourages empathy with others.

Materials

A4 sheet of cartridge paper

Soft or plastic eraser

Pencil sharpener

HB, 2B and 4B pencils

Ruler

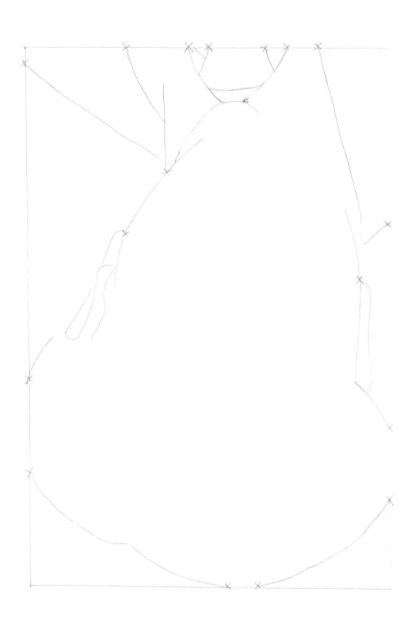

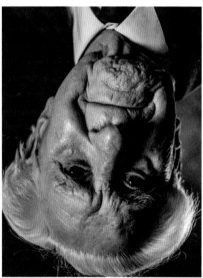

Photograph © Mike Coles

The first task, with the HB pencil, is to draw a frame twice the size of the portrait illustrated, using a ruler to get straight parallel lines.

Identify some of the key points at the edges of the photo, such as where the subject's shoulder meets the frame. With your ruler, measure the distance of this point from the corner and double it. Measure this dimension on your paper and mark it with a small cross – you are effectively scaling the image by a factor of two. Work around the edges first, and then identify, measure and mark some of the key points in the middle of the picture, for example, where the ears are placed, and the edges of the tie and jacket.

Lightly sketch in the outline of the face, using the crosses as a guide. Gradually, the upside-down head shape will emerge.

2 Measure and plot the corners of the mouth, the corners of the eyes, the widest part of the nostrils and the point where the deep fold in the chin meets the face. Using these points, draw in more of the portrait until it is fully mapped out.

3 Lightly hatch in the first layer of tone, still using the HB pencil. Don't worry
too much about the direction of your hatching as it will be overlaid in the next
two stages. Try half-closing your eyes to help identify the main areas of tone in
the background, on the jacket, and on the face around the eyes, hair, mouth and
nose. Add in a few lines and some light tone to indicate the direction of the hair
and eyebrows.

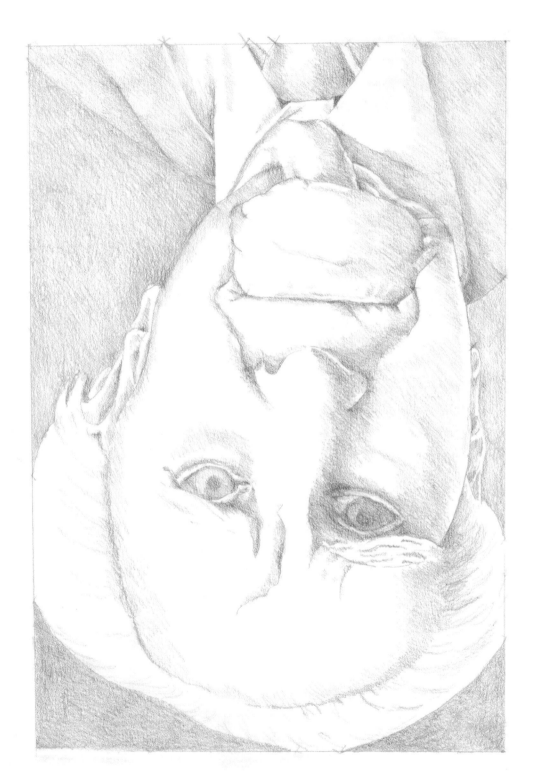

4   Using a 2B pencil, add more tone, gradually building up the density. Aim
     to darken the background and jacket as well as the features on the face. The
range of tones will begin to give the face more depth. You can erase some of the
measurement crosses at this stage.

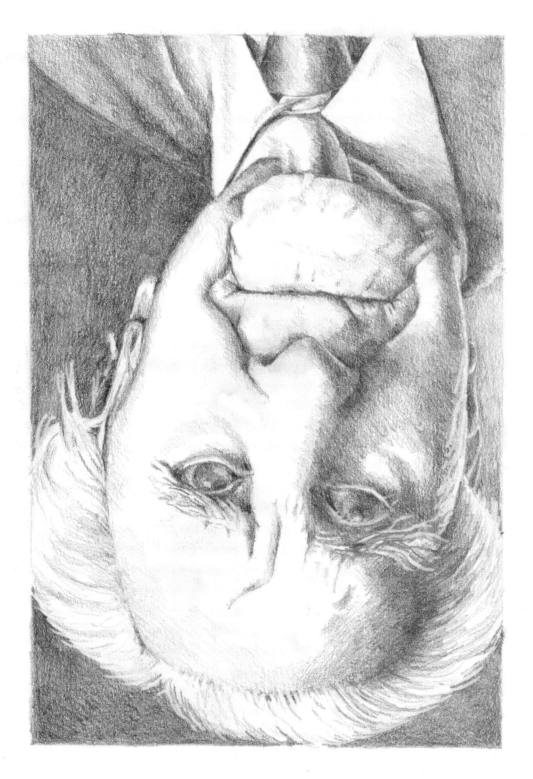

5 Switch to a 4B pencil to add more layers of tone, aiming to increase the contrast to complete the drawing. Varying the pressure of the pencil on the paper should achieve a blended effect – don't try to smudge a pencil drawing as it tends to look messy. You can use an eraser to reinstate any highlights that you may accidentally cover. Only now can you turn the drawing the right way round.

Here you can compare the original photograph to the finished drawing to see the result of your efforts. My students really enjoy upside-down drawing and are often very surprised by the accuracy of the end result. Many begin this exercise doubting both their abilities and my confidence in them, but they are invariably won over in the end.

Photograph © Mike Coles

Tempted to make more portraits?

This upside-down technique means that you don't have to use generally accepted facial proportions. However, if the exercise has given you the confidence to try drawing a portrait the right way round, the following guidelines may be helpful:

- The eyes are about halfway down the head.
- The bottom of the nose is roughly midway between the eyes and the mouth.
- The left and right eyes are about one eye-width apart.
- The outer edges of the nostrils align with the inner corners of the eyes.
- The outer corners of the mouth align with the pupils of the eyes.
- The tops of the ears roughly align with the eyes.

Abstract Circles

Make a bold statement with drawing inks

In this exercise you will experiment with coloured drawing inks to make an abstract image. The colours of the inks are strong and rich compared with watercolours, and their 'transparency' is reminiscent of stained-glass windows, especially after black outlines have been added.

I have used a high white watercolour paper as this enhances the luminosity and vibrancy of the inks. It also has the advantage of not cockling when the paint is applied, which could happen on a lighter-weight cartridge paper. An initial painting plan is essential as after the inks have been applied to the paper, unlike watercolour paint, they are almost impossible to remove.

This painting consists of a repeat pattern of circles placed within a grid – it may sound a bit technical, but you should find it straightforward if you follow the stages overleaf. You may find a battery-operated eraser is useful here as it has the advantage of being able to remove smaller areas of pencil than a conventional eraser. Once the grid is drawn you can fill in the resulting shapes using a selection of coloured inks, ensuring that no two adjacent shapes have the same colour. Making an abstract composition can be very liberating, as you don't have the expectation of trying to depict a 'real' subject. You can simply follow your instincts and concentrate fully on form and colour.

You should find this an easy and enjoyable exercise, and the vibrant colours can produce a very cheering effect. Over the years I have acquired a large selection of coloured inks which has given me plenty of choice, but you can manage quite well with a limited number. If you are planning to try the butterfly exercise on pages 90–7, you could buy inks that will be used in both projects. This exercise can also be done in watercolour paint but the result will not be so rich and vibrant.

Therapeutic benefits

- Colouring in can evoke memories of drawing as a child
- Bright, vibrant colours are uplifting
- Abstract designs can be liberating and expressive
- An easy and absorbing exercise that can be repeated with different colours
- A great sense of achievement from mastering the drawing of the template
- Especially enjoyable for those with an interest in geometric patterns.

Materials

½ imperial (38 x 56cm/15 x 22in) 300gsm (140lb) NOT watercolour paper

HB pencil

Soft or plastic eraser

Ruler

No. 10, No. 6 and No. 2 round watercolour brushes

Saucer, about 12cm (5in) diameter

Selection of glasses, spice jars, coins, about 5.5cm, 4.5cm, 2.5cm and 2cm (2in, 1¾in, 1in and ¾in) diameter

Faber-Castell Pitt Artist Fineliner Pen black size B (brush) or a similar waterproof black fibre-tip pen

Drawing Inks

Winsor & Newton range

Canary Yellow

Orange

Violet

Scarlet

Carmine

Blue

Purple

Emerald

Black

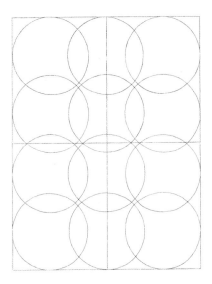

1 Use a pencil throughout Stages 1 to 3 (I have used pen here to show the design clearly). Draw a rectangle measuring 30 x 40cm (12 x 16in) on your paper with a pencil and ruler. Use the straight edges of the paper to help achieve a reasonably true rectangle. Draw lines through the centres of the two sides – 15cm (6in) is the mid-point along the shorter edge and 20cm (8in) is the middle of the longer edge. You should have four rectangles, all the same size, as in the example.

2 The next step is to fill the rectangle with overlapping circles, using the saucer as a template (or a pair of compasses if you prefer). Place two circles snugly in the two corners at the top end of the rectangle. Draw two more circles at the bottom end of the rectangle in the same way, then place a third circle in the middle of the two pairs of circles, centred on the grid line.

You should now have three overlapping circles at the top and bottom of the rectangle. Next, position two more circles along each long edge of the rectangle. One side of each circle should touch the long edge and the other should overlap the adjacent circles by about 3cm (1¼in). Draw the final two middle circles, again to give about 3cm (1¼in) overlaps. Don't worry if the overlaps aren't exactly the same – it will all add to the interest of the final artwork. You should now have 12 overlapping circles as in the example.

3 Now draw the smaller circles within the larger ones, using your smaller templates. You can position them well enough by eye if you look carefully at the size of the spaces between the larger circles drawn in Stage 2 – don't worry if they're not exactly centred. I drew round a couple of glasses and as they were transparent I could see where to position the inner circles within the outer circles. Lastly I added in a square at each end with a circle inside it. The square measures 4 x 4cm (1½ x 1½in), which happened to be the same size as the ink bottle box, providing the perfect template to draw round.

4 Erase unwanted pencil lines, such as the two central grid lines. Give your paper a gentle sweep with a
   soft brush to remove any debris that may have come from the eraser. This is often not apparent until
you start painting and it may interfere with the smoothness of the ink.

   Start the painting by placing in all the yellow shapes, followed by the orange and violet. Take care to
ensure each area is dry before you paint near it as you need to avoid smudging the wet ink. It does dry
fairly quickly. Use the No. 10 brushes for the larger areas, No. 6 for smaller areas and No. 2 for the more
fiddly details. Be as careful as you can to keep the edges neat and tidy. Wash your brushes thoroughly
when changing colours.

5 Paint in the remaining colours – purple, emerald, scarlet, carmine, blue and black. When you are
sure the inks are all dry use the fibre-tip pen to outline the shapes you have created in freehand – if
you work slowly and methodically, with your hand resting firmly on the paper, you should find this
straightforward. This will not only enhance the brightness of the colours, it will also tidy up any rough
edges between the colours. You should now have an exciting, vibrant design which suggests movement
and rhythm from the overlapping circles.

As an extension exercise you could see what happens if you substitute the colour scheme with
harmonious colours such as greens, blues and yellow. Referring back to the colour wheel exercises (pages
34–5), try adding an accent colour such as red in the smallest shapes in the pattern to see the dramatic
effect it has on the adjacent colours and the overall design.